AMERICAN CUTTING EDGE

LEVEL 2

Longman

The English Language Training College

WORKBOOK

peter moor   sarah cunningham

Contents

module 1

Names and countries

1 **a)** Complete the conversation with words from the box.

| ~~My~~ this your Hello you name 's Nice And What |

SEBASTIAN: Hello. (1) ...*My*............... name (2) ....
Sebastian. (3) ....'s (4) .... name?

FLORENCE: My (5) ....'s Florence.

SEBASTIAN: (6) .... to meet (7) ...., Florence.

FLORENCE: (8) .... you.

SEBASTIAN: And (9) .... is my friend, Charlotte.

FLORENCE: Hello, Charlotte.

CHARLOTTE: (10) ....

b) 📼 Listen and repeat the conversation.

Personal information: *be*

2 Write the questions and answers.

a) Jim Carrey – the US

1 *What's his name?*
2 *His name's Jim Carrey.*
3 *Where's he from?*
4 *He's from the US.*

b) Gisele Bundchen – Brazil

1 What ....?
2 Her ....
3 Where ....?
4 She ....

c) Andrea, Jim, Caroline, and Sharon Corr – Ireland

1 What ....?
2 Their ....
3 Where ....?
4 They ....

d) Venus Williams – the US

1 ....?
2 ....
3 ....?
4 ....

e) David and Victoria Beckham – England

1 ....?
2 ....
3 ....?
4 ....

f) Roberto Benigni – Italy

1 ....?
2 ....
3 ....?
4 ....

is or are

3 Complete the sentences with *is* or *are*.

a My name ...*is*........ Martina.

b Where .... you from?

c .... Walter from Germany?

d He .... 22 years old.

e .... Ross and Jennifer married?

f .... you on vacation?

g Fernanda .... a Spanish teacher.

Negative sentences

4 Make the sentences negative.

a Edinburgh ~~is~~ *isn't* in England.

b I'm from Ireland.

c My mother and father are English.

d Brazil is a small country.

e My name is Lana.

f My sister is married.

g I'm 15 years old.

h Philip and Elizabeth are on vacation.

Personal questions: *be*

5 **a)** Choose a word from Column B to complete each question.

Column A	Column B
1 What's your ...*name*........?	~~student~~
2 How are ....?	~~brothers~~
3 How old are your ....?	~~Michelle~~
4 Are you a ....?	English
5 Is David ....?	~~you~~
6 Is your name ....?	~~vacation~~
7 Where are they ....?	~~name~~
8 Are they on ....?	~~from~~

b) 📼 Listen to the questions on the recording. Practice saying them.

Short answers

6 Write the short answers for the questions.

a Are you Portuguese?
No, *I'm not*........................ . I'm Brazilian.

b Is James English?
Yes, ... He's from Manchester.

c Is your address 16 New Street?
No, ... It's 26 New Road.

d Are you and your friend here on vacation?
No, ... We're here on business.

e Is Barbara married?
Yes, ... Her husband's a doctor.

f Are you married?
Yes, ... This is my husband, James.

g Is Thomas an actor?
No, ... He's a musician.

h Are Anne and Michael English?
No, ... They're from Ireland.

i Is "Howard" your surname?
Yes, ... My first name's Tony.

j Is Jacqueline a teacher?
No, ... She's a student.

Possessive adjectives

7 Look at the pictures and complete the sentences with *my*, *your*, *his*, *her*, *our*, or *their*.

Hi! (a) ..*My*............... name's Ed ... Ed Turner! And this is (b) .... wife. (c) .... name's Thelma. This is (d) .... beautiful house!!

This is Thelma with (e) .... two children – (f) .... names are Bob and Tracey – and (g) .... brother – (h) .... name's Louis.

And this is (i) .... dog ... what's (j) .... name, friend?

(k) .... name's Bones.

Indefinite article: *a(n)*

8 Write *a* or *an*.

a ..*an*.......... actor
b .... manager
c .... email address
d .... lesson
e .... telephone number
f .... vacation
g .... teacher
h .... English teacher

Vocabulary

Jobs

9 Rearrange the mixed-up letters to make words for jobs.

a r a c t o   ..*actor*...............
b r a w e i t   ....
c e c l i p o   c o i f f e r   ....
d a n u m i s i c   ....
e c r e a t e h   ....
f s t o n p r a m s ....
g s i t t a r   ....
h r o c d o t   ....

Vocabulary booster: countries and nationalities

10 **a)** Write the nationalities.

Country	Nationality
1 Australia	*Australian*........
2 Brazil	....
3 Italy	....
4 England	....
5 Spain	....
6 Scotland	....
7 France	....
8 the US	....

b) 🔊 Listen and practice saying the words.

Listen and read

11 🔲 Listen and read about four people. Who:

a is an actress? *Béatrice Santini*

b is a taxi driver? ....

c is from France? ....

d are musicians? ....

e is from London? ....

f is from Edinburgh? ....

g is a bus driver? ....

h is 45 years old? ....

People from different places

Béatrice Santini

Béatrice Santini is from France. She's 28 years old, and she's an actress. She's married; her husband is movie director Karol Bolewski. Karol is 56 years old. Their home is in Paris.

Donna Fiorelli

Donna Fiorelli is from New York. She's a taxi driver. She's 45 years old. Is she married? "Yes, I am ... I'm married to my job."

Magnus Mills

"Hello. My name is Magnus Mills. I'm 37 years old, and I'm single. I'm a bus driver in London. I'm also a writer: my first book is *Bus Driver on Holiday*."

Plankton

Allan, Doug, Richard, and Kirsty are Plankton ... four musicians from Aberdeen, in Scotland. Their manager is Betty Booth. Betty is from Edinburgh, and she's 25 years old.

Punctuation: capital letters

> **LOOK!**
>
> We use capital letters for:
>
> – names   *Lara Croft*
> – countries   *China*
> – nationalities *Brazilian*
> – roads   *Fifth Avenue*
> – towns/cities   *Istanbul*

12 Write the capital letters.

a his name's graham smith.
   His name's Graham Smith................

b my mother's from the united states.
   ....

c are you spanish?
   ....

d our school is on camden road.
   ....

e i'm from rome.
   ....

f eric lives in berlin.
   ....

Improve your writing

Addresses in English

13 **a)** Look at the address on this envelope.

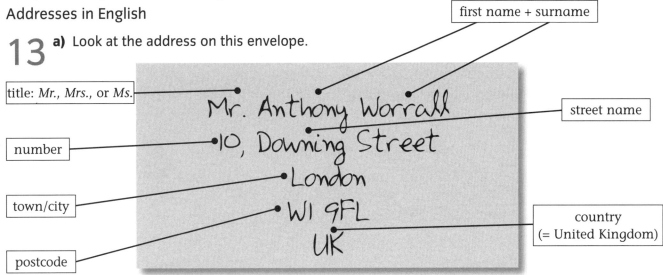

first name + surname

title: *Mr., Mrs.,* or *Ms.*

street name

number

town/city

country (= United Kingdom)

postcode

Mr. Anthony Worrall
10, Downing Street
London
W1 9FL
UK

b) Write these addresses in the correct order.

1 SW15 6GS – South London College – UK – London – Richmond Road – 52

....

....

....

....

....

2 Dublin – 4 – Ireland – Mary Burke – Mrs. – 109 St. Stephen Street

....

....

....

....

....

c) Write the capital letters.

miss sarah ellis ....

62 high street ....

amersham ....

hp7 0dj ....

england ....

mr. simon henderson ....

12 muirfield road ....

glasgow ....

g12 8sj ....

scotland ....

Pronunciation

/ɑː/, /eɪ/, and /aɪ/

14 **a)** 🔊 Listen to the pronunciation of these words. Practice saying them.

/ɑː/	/eɪ/	/aɪ/
on	name	I
body	age	fine
father	they	my

b) 🔊 Listen to the words. Write /ɑː/, /eɪ/, or /aɪ/.

1 write /......aɪ......./

2 eight /.............../

3 job /.............../

4 doctor /.............../

5 nine /.............../

6 Spain /.............../

7 nice /.............../

8 not /.............../

module 2

Identifying objects: *this*, *that*, *these*, *those*

1 Describe the pictures, using *this*, *that*, *these*, or *those*.

a ..*this*........ car

b .... shoes

c .... boy

d .... coat

e .... chairs

f .... men

g .... women

h .... book

a/an or Ø with objects and plurals

2 What's in the bag? Write *a*, *an*, or Ø.

a ......*a*........ cellphone
b .... apple
c .... English dictionary
d .... camera
e .... address book
f .... keys
g .... comb
h .... photos
i .... datebook
j .... identity card

(do) have/don't have

3 **a)** Read the information in the table. Complete the sentences with *has*, *doesn't/have*, or *don't have/*

	Silvia	Martin and Inge	Alfonso
Pet?	dog (Rex)	no	two cats
Car?	yes – an Audi	two	no
Computer?	no	yes	yes

1 Silvia *has* .... a dog – his name's Rex.

2 She .... a car – it's an Audi.

3 She .... a computer.

4 Martin and Inge .... a pet.

5 They .... two cars.

6 They .... a computer.

7 Alfonso .... two cats.

8 He .... a car.

9 He .... a computer.

b) 🔊 Listen and check your answers. Practice saying the sentences.

Questions and short answers

LOOK!

Do I/you/ we/they **have**	a dog? a car?	**Yes**, I/you/ we **do**. **No**, I/you/ we **don't**.
Does he/she/ it **have**	a computer?	**Yes**, he/she/ it **does**. **No**, he/she/ it **doesn't**.

4 **a)** Look back at the information about Silvia, Alfonso, and Martin and Inge, and complete the questions and answers below.

1 *Does*...... Silvia *have*........ a dog?
   Yes, she does. ....

2 .... she .... a car?
   ....

3 .... she .... a computer?
   ....

4 .... Martin and Inge .... a pet?
   ....

5 .... they .... a car?
   ....

6 .... they .... a computer?
   ....

7 .... Alfonso .... a pet?
   ....

8 .... he .... a car?
   ....

9 .... he .... a computer?
   ....

b) 🔊 Listen and check your answers. Practice saying the sentences.

Adjectives and nouns

> **LOOK!**
>
> **Adjectives:**
>
> – go **before** nouns   *a comfortable car*
> – do **not** change   *blue eyes*
> – do **not** use *and*   *a large red hat*

5 Put the adjective in the correct place in the sentences.

a Max has a car – it's a BMW. (*German*)
   Max has a German car - it's a BMW. ....

b Your dog has eyes. (*beautiful*)
   ....

c We have two cats at home. (*black*)
   ....

d I have a computer game – *Crash 5!!!* (*fantastic*)
   ....

e My friend Al is a musician. (*professional*)
   ....

f Lauren Bacall is my actress. (*favorite*)
   ....

g My sister has a cellphone. (*new*)
   ....

h Goldie is a dog. (*friendly*)
   ....

Vocabulary booster: more everyday objects

6 **a)** Label the objects in the picture with words from the box.

> a passport   an address book   a hairbrush
> car keys   a calculator   a pen   a pencil   a mirror
> a tube of lipstick   a pack of chewing gum

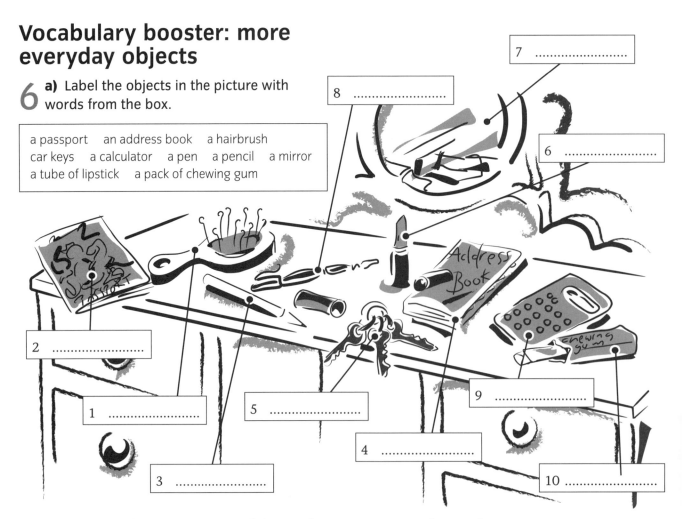

7 ....

8 ....

6 ....

2 ....

1 ....

5 ....

9 ....

4 ....

3 ....

10 ....

b) 🎧 Listen to the pronunciation of the words. Practice saying the words.

Vocabulary

Relationship vocabulary

7 a) Look at the picture and information about The Doyle Family.

Brenda Doyle – Joe's wife

Joe Doyle – "Dad"

Jason Doyle – Jane's brother

Colin Best – Jane's husband

Jane Best – Joe and Brenda's daughter

Nora Walker (Nana) – Brenda's mother

The Doyle Family

b) Use the information to complete the sentences.

1 Joe Doyle is Brenda's *husband.* .

2 Jason is Joe and Brenda's ....

3 Brenda is Jane and Jason's ....

4 Joe is their ....

5 Joe and Brenda are Jane's ....

6 Colin is Jane's ....

c) Answer the questions with two sentences, as in the example.

1 Who is Nora Walker?

  She's Brenda's mother.

  She's Jane and Jason's grandmother.

2 Who is Jason?

  ....

  ....

3 Who is Joe?

  ....

  ....

4 Who is Brenda?

  ....

  ....

5 Who is Jane?

  ....

  ....

6 Who are Jane and Jason?

  ....

  ....

Listen and read

8 **a)** 🔲 Read and listen to the text about the Iglesias family.

A Famous Family

Julio Iglesias is from Spain. The world's number 1 Spanish singer in the 70s and 80s, with songs like *Begin the Beguine*, he is now the father of a famous family. The three children from his marriage in the 1970s to actress Isabel Preysler – two sons and a daughter – are now all famous too.

His daughter, Chaveli, is a TV presenter in the United States. His sons' names are Julio Junior and Enrique: Julio Junior is a model, actor, and singer. His songs are in English and Spanish.

Enrique Iglesias is also a singer. His home is in Miami, Florida. He's got two Porsche cars at home!!

b) Complete the information in the family tree about the Iglesias family.

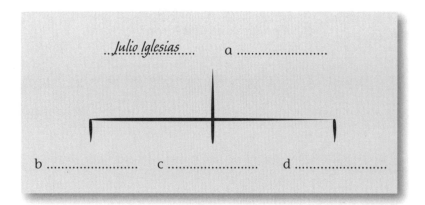

..*Julio Iglesias*.... a ....

b .... c .... d ....

Possessive 's

9 Write 's in the correct place in the sentences, as in the example.

a Patrick is Jane's brother.

b Is that Michael car?

c It's Tessa birthday on Saturday.

d What's your mother name?

e Where's Philip desk?

f My husband name is Peter.

g Jo is my sister friend.

h Carla house is in downtown Rome.

Spelling

Plurals

10 **a)** Write the plural of these words.

1 datebook ...*datebooks*.........

2 dictionary ....

3 box ....

4 college ....

5 baby ....

6 key ....

7 match ....

8 watch ....

9 house ....

10 bus ....

11 address ....

12 boy ....

b) Rearrange the mixed-up letters to make irregular plurals.

1 h c r n e i l d ...*children*.........

2 v s i w e ....

3 e f t e ....

4 n e m ....

5 e n o w m ....

6 s i l e v ....

Pronunciation

The sounds /s/ and /z/

11 **a)** 🔊 Listen to the pronunciation of the /s/ sound. Underline the /s/ sounds.

What's this?

– It's my passport.

b) 🔊 Listen to the pronunciation of the /z/ sound. Circle the /z/ sounds.

His friend's name is James.

c) 🔊 Listen. Underline the /s/ sounds.

1 This is my sister. Her name's Suzanne.

2 Those are my keys!

3 She's seven years old.

4 What's his address?

5 She has fantastic blue eyes.

6 What's your brother's first name?

7 Sarah is a famous actress.

8 What's the answer to this question?

d) 🔊 Listen again. Circle the /z/ sounds.

Prepositions

12 Underline the correct preposition.

a What's that *at/in* English?

b Do you have your datebook *for/with* you?

c We have two dogs *at/in* my family.

d John is a student *at/for* Cambridge University.

e We have cable TV *at/to* home.

f I have a pen *in/on* my bag.

Improve your writing

Writing about people in your family

13 **a)** Read about the people in this family.

People in my family

My father's name is Martin Hancock. He's fifty-three years old and he's an architect. He and my mother aren't married now – they're divorced. His new wife's name is Judy. They have a baby daughter – her name's Cassandra and she's beautiful!!!

My sister, Caroline, is twenty-eight years old, and she's a teacher. She's married. Her husband's name is Marcos – he's from Chile. They have two daughters: Rebecca, who's five, and Annabel, who's two years old. I'm their aunt!!

My cousin Martha is from Australia. She's nineteen years old, and she isn't married: she's a student at the University of Melbourne. She has a boyfriend – his name is Mark. He's twenty. He isn't a student: he's a professional musician. The name of his group is MC2.

My grandmother is about eighty years old. Her name is Beatrice. She has six children – four sons and two daughters – and she has twenty-three grandchildren!!

b) Write sentences about some people in your family.

e.g.: *My father's name is Karl.*

My sister, Marjana, is twenty years old.

15

module 3

Present Simple

Questions

1 **a)** Complete the questions with words from the box.

soccer   in   Do   French   like   study   ~~live~~   you

1   Do you ....*live*.......... in Edinburgh?

2   .... your parents speak English?

3   Do you and your brother like ....?

4   Do .... like Japanese tea, Johnny?

5   Do Sophie and Emily speak ....?

6   Do you all .... economics?

7   Does the White family live .... an apartment?

8   Do you .... Indian food, Paula?

b) 🖭 Listen to the questions on the recording. Practice saying them.

Negatives

2 **a)** Join the two halves to make negative sentences.

1   People in Brazil don't speak   to school.
2   Cats don't like   in the morning.
3   Most people don't go to work   Spanish.
4   Babies don't go   water.
5   Banks in Britain don't close   rock music.
6   Most restaurants don't open   on Sunday.
7   My grandparents don't like   at lunchtime.

b) 🖭 Listen to the sentences on the recording. Practice saying them.

Positive and negative

3 **a)** Read the information about Thomas and Angela, from Sweden, and Julia and Gregg, from Singapore.

Thomas and Angela   **Julia and Gregg**

from	a small town in Sweden	Singapore City
house	5-bedroom house	a small apartment in Singapore City
languages	Swedish, English, German	English, Chinese, Malay
likes	classical music, skiing	Chinese food
dislikes	smoking	heavy metal music
drinks	mineral water and coffee	tea and coffee

b) Complete the sentences.

1 Thomas and Angela *don't live* .... in a big city.

2 They .... in a big house.

3 They .... English.

4 They .... Chinese.

5 They .... classical music.

6 They .... smoking.

7 They .... mineral water.

8 They .... tea.

9 Julia and Gregg ...... *live* .... in a big city.

10 They .... in a big house.

11 They .... Chinese and English.

12 They .... German.

13 They .... Chinese food.

14 They .... heavy metal music.

15 They .... milk.

16 They .... tea.

Questions and short answers

4 Answer the questions about Thomas, Angela, Julia, and Gregg with short answers. Then answer the questions about yourself.

a Do Thomas and Angela live in a
small town?   *Yes, they do.*
Do you live in a small town?   *No, I don't.*

b Do they like classical music?   ....
Do you like classical music?   ....

c Do they speak Chinese?   ....
Do you speak Chinese?   ....

d Do they drink tea?   ....
Do you drink tea?   ....

e Do Julia and Gregg live in a big city? ....
Do you live in a big city?   ....

f Do they speak German?   ....
Do you speak German?   ....

g Do they like heavy metal music?   ....
Do you like heavy metal music?   ....

h Do they drink milk?   ....
Do you drink milk?   ....

Subject and object pronouns

5

LOOK!

I, *you*, *he*, *she*, *it*, *we*, and *they* are **subject pronouns**.

me, *you*, *him*, *her*, *it*, *us*, and *them* are **object pronouns**.

subject pronoun		object pronoun
I	⇨	me
you	⇨	you
he	⇨	him
she	⇨	her
it	⇨	it
we	⇨	us
they	⇨	them

We use **object pronouns**:
* after prepositions
  *come with **me***
* when the pronoun is the object of the sentence
  *Sarah loves **him***

Correct the pronouns in **bold**, as in the example.

a Is your ice cream OK? Do you like ~~them~~? *it*

b Is that your sister?
– Yes, it is ... but who's that with **she**?

c We've got a big apartment, and my grandparents live with **we**.

d Is that letter for **I**?

e What's her name?
– Karen.
How do you spell **her**?

f Is Peter Martin your boyfriend?
– No!! I don't like **he**!!!

g Do you like the Spice Girls?
– Yes, I do. I love **they**!!

h What's Julia's address?
– I don't know ... I haven't got **him** with **I**.

Vocabulary

Collocations with common verbs

6 Write three words or phrases from the box with each verb below.

in an apartment   tea   to school   ~~Japanese~~   law   English grammar ~~French~~   mineral water   a snack   home   in a house   ~~Spanish~~   milk a meal   to college   breakfast   economics   in a city

a speak ..._French_.... , ..._Spanish_.... , ..._Japanese_......

b drink .... , ... , ...

c live .... , ... , ...

d have .... , ... , ...

e go .... , ... , ...

f study .... , ... , ...

Vocabulary booster: buildings

7 **a)** Label the buildings with words from the box.

~~an apartment house~~   a library   a school   a bank   a supermarket a railroad station   a hospital   a hotel

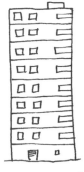

1 _an apartment house_

2 ....

3 ....

4 ....

5 ....

6 ....

7 ....

8 ....

b) 🖭 Listen to the pronunciation of the words. Practice saying them.

Listen and read

8 a) 📼 Read and listen to the text about young people in South Korea.

Studying in South Korea
....

What time do you have breakfast?
Where do you have lunch?
Do you go out with your friends for a cup of coffee after school or after work?
Do you work in the evenings, or do you have dinner with family or friends?

Life is very different for many young people in South Korea. It's very important for people to go to a good college, and find a good job ... so studying is very, very important! Young people get up at about six o'clock, have breakfast with their family, and then go to school ... schools in South Korea start at seven o'clock.

After five hours of lessons in the morning, it's time for lunch. Most people have lunch at school. Then there are more lessons until six o'clock ... but that's not the end! Many young Koreans go to the library and study from about eight o'clock to eleven or twelve o'clock, when the libraries close.

At that time, they go home in a special minibus. Most students don't go to bed before one or two o'clock, and then the next day, after just four or five hours of sleep, it's time to get up again!

b) Answer these questions.

1 What time do most young people get up in South Korea?
   They get up at about six o'clock.

2 What time do schools open in South Korea?
   ....

3 Where do young people have lunch?
   ....

4 What time do schools in South Korea finish?
   ....

5 Where do many young people go in the evening?
   ....

6 What time do the libraries close?
   ....

7 How do people go home?
   ....

8 What time do they go to bed?
   ....

Prepositions: *in*, *at*, or *to*

9 Complete the sentences with *in*, *at*, or *to*.

a It's seven o'clock ..*in*.......... the morning.

b He's got an apartment .... Essen, a big city .... Germany.

c What time do you go .... bed?

d Is the restaurant open .... the afternoon?

e Do you work .... a bank?

f My brother Frank is .... college.

g Where do you go .... school?

h Do you live .... a big house?

i Most stores close .... lunchtime.

j The stores close .... ten o'clock .... the evening.

Opposites

10 Rearrange the letters to make opposites.

a finish
   a r t s t   ....

b morning   *start*
   v i n e n e g   ....

c go to bed
   t e g p u   ....

d open
   s o l c e   ....

e go to work
   m o c e m e h o m o r f k r o w
   ....

Pronunciation

The letter *i*

11 **a)** 📼 We pronounce the letter *i* in different ways.
Listen to these examples.

/ɪ/   live, city

/aɪ/   I, like

b) Look at the words in the box. Do we pronounce *i* as /ɪ/ or as /aɪ/? Put the words into the correct column.

| drink   six   big   finish   life   this   nine   time |
| five   children   write   listen   night   dinner |

/ɪ/	/aɪ/
drink	*time*
....	....
....	....
....	....
....	....
....	....
....	

c) 📼 Listen to the pronunciation of the words. Practice saying them.

Improve your writing

Commas, periods, *and*, and *but*

,	a comma	LOOK!
.	a period	
linkers	*and*, *but*	

12 **a)** Write three commas, a period, and a linker in the sentence below.

In Britain children start school at about nine o'clock in the morning in Poland they start school at eight o'clock

b) Use the information in the box to write sentences about the differences between life in New York and life in York, a town in the north of England. Use commas, periods, *and*, or *but*.

	New York, USA	York, UK
Most people live in	apartments	houses
Most people start work	8 a.m.	9 a.m.
Most people finish work	6 p.m.	5:30 p.m.
Children start school at	5 years	4 years
Most stores open at	9 a.m.	9 a.m.
Most stores close at	8 p.m.	6 p.m.

1 (New York/live/York/live)

   In New York, most people live in apartments, but in York, most people live in houses.

2 (New York/start work/finish work)

   In New York, most people start work at 8 a.m., and they finish work at 6 p.m.

3 (New York/start work/York)

   ....

4 (York/start work/finish work)

   ....

5 (New York/finish work/York)

   ....

6 (New York/children start school/York)

   ....

7 (New York/stores open/close)

   ....

8 (New York/stores close/York)

   ....

too, *both*, and *neither*

LOOK!

We use *me, too* to agree with a positive sentence.
A: *I love Chinese food.*
B: *Me, too!!*

We use *me, neither* to agree with a negative sentence.
A: *I'm not tired.*
B: *Me, neither.*

We use *both* to say that two things or people are the same. Notice the position of *both*.
*We **both** like jazz.*
*They are **both** nineteen years old.*

13 Write *both*, *neither*, or *too* in the sentences.

a Are you from the US?
   – Yes, I'm from California.
   Oh really? Me, *too*..........!

b Paula and her sister are
   .... teachers.

c I don't like jazz.
   – Me, ...

d We're here on vacation. How
   about you?
   – Yes, me, ...

e I don't understand this
   movie. – Me, ...

f Nick and I .... work at
   the Bridge Hotel.

g I don't take milk in my
   coffee.
   – No, me, ...

h Stefan loves basketball.
   – Me, ...!

module 4

Present Simple

Spelling

1 Write the letters to make the *he/she/it* form.

a My mother read_s_ *Hi!* magazine.

b James watch_ _ TV in the morning.

c Winnie come_ from South Korea.

d Richard live_ in the United States.

e She go_ _ to bed at eleven o'clock.

f Francis enjoy_ watching soccer on TV.

g My brother say_ he's fine.

h Norma stud_ _ _ economics at the University of Leeds.

i Ian always play_ soccer on Saturday.

Present Simple with *he/she/it*

2 a) Look at the information in the chart and complete these sentences about Akiko Murata.

1 She ..*comes*............... from Japan. (*come*)

2 She .... fashion design. (*study*)

3 She .... in San Francisco. (*live*)

4 She .... Japanese and English. (*speak*)

5 She .... cooking and ballet. (*like*)

	Nationality	Job	Address	Languages	Hobbies
Akiko Murata	Japanese	fashion design student	Golden Gate Ave., San Francisco, USA	Japanese, English	cooking, ballet
David Jones	British	English teacher	The English School, Seoul, South Korea	English, French, Korean	watching soccer, playing the guitar
Beatriz Ayala	Argentinian	bank employee	Carrer Bonavista, Barcelona, Spain	Spanish, Catalan, English	painting, going to the gym
Zoltán Tarnai	Hungarian	music teacher	Rue d'Alleray, Paris, France	Hungarian, French, German	playing tennis, walking

b) 🖭 Listen to the sentences. Practice saying them.

c) Write sentences about David, Beatriz, and Zoltán using the Present Simple.

1 *David Jones teaches English.*...................... (*teach*)

2 He .... (*come from*)

3 .... (*live*)

4 .... (*speak*)

5 .... (*play*)

6 *Beatriz Ayala lives in Spain.*...................... (*live*)

7 She .... (*come from*)

8 .... (*speak*)

9 .... (*work*)

10 .... (*go to the gym*)

11 *Zoltán Tarnai speaks Hungarian, French,............... and German.*...................... (*speak*)

12 He .... (*come from*)

13 .... (*live*)

14 .... (*teach*)

15 .... (*play*)

Short answers

3 a) Look at the information about Akiko and David on page 22 and write the correct short answers.

1 Does Akiko come from Japan? *Yes, she does.*
2 Does she study economics? *No, she doesn't.*
3 Does she live in New York? ....
4 Does she speak English? ....
5 Does she like ballet? ....
6 Does David come from the US? ....
7 Does he teach English? ....
8 Does he live in South Korea? ....
9 Does he speak Chinese? ....
10 Does he play tennis? ....

b) 📼 Listen to the questions and answers on the recording. Practice saying them.

Negatives

4 a) Make these sentences negative.

1 Maria likes studying grammar.
   Maria doesn't like studying grammar.

2 It rains in summer.
   ....

3 My brother likes getting up at seven o'clock.
   ....

4 The restaurant closes on Sunday evening.
   ....

5 Martin comes to class every week.
   ....

6 Tony buys all his food at the supermarket.
   ....

7 Carla drives to work.
   ....

8 My cousin visits me every month.
   ....

b) 📼 Listen to the sentences. Practice saying them.

Positives and negatives

5 Put the verb into the correct form of the Present Simple.

Malcolm Tracey (a) ..*doesn't go*.. (*not/go*) to work: he only (b) .... (*leave*) his home town to go on vacation in the Caribbean with his family. But Malcolm is a millionaire. He (c) .... (*write*) books about money, and how to make a lot of it. His new book is called *Easy Money: How to make money without getting out of bed*. Malcolm (d) .... (*live*) in a large house in Bray, a town about 40 kilometers from London. He (e) .... (*get up*) at about nine o'clock in the morning, and (f) .... (*have*) breakfast with his family. After breakfast, he (g) .... (*drive*) his children to school in his white Rolls-Royce, and (h) .... (*read*) the newspaper in his yard until lunchtime. After lunch, he (i) .... (*buy*) and (j) .... (*sell*) on the Internet. He (k) .... (*finish*) work at four o'clock when his children come home. "I have a simple system for making money," Malcolm (l) .... (*say*). "It (m) .... (*not work*) for everybody ... but it (n) .... (*work*) for me!!"

Questions

6 Write questions about Malcolm Tracey.

a (Where/live) *Where does he live?* ....
....
In Bray.

b (When/get up) ....
....
At nine o'clock in the morning.

c (What/do/after breakfast) ....
He drives his children to school.

d (Where/read the newspaper) ....
In the yard.

e (Where/go on vacation) ....
To the Caribbean.

f (What/do after lunch) ....
He buys and sells on the Internet.

g (What time/finish work)..
At four o'clock.

Adverbs of frequency

7 Underline the true sentence.

a In the morning, the sun *always/never/sometimes* rises in the east.

b Sharks *never/sometimes/often* kill people.

c Children *never/don't often/usually* like candy.

d In the game of chess, black *always/never/usually* starts.

e People with brown hair *don't often/never/often* have brown eyes.

f Monday *always/often/usually* comes before Tuesday.

g A year *always/never/usually* has 364 days.

h Spiders *always/often/sometimes* have eight legs.

Activity verbs

8 Complete the sentences with verbs from the box.

| read write watch listen |
| plays go visit study |
| write read go listen |

a Do you ..*read*............. the newspaper every day?
– No, I don't. I only ..*read*............. magazines.

b Do you ever .... swimming on weekends?
– No, I don't, but I often .... shopping!

c My mother and father always .... a video on a Friday night.

d I usually .... to a CD when I drive to work. I never .... to the radio.

e My brother Hector loves sports: he .... rugby, basketball, tennis, and chess!!

f I never .... letters: but I .... a lot of emails!!

g I always .... my friend Roger when I'm in London.

h I'm a student at Edinburgh University.
– What do you ....?
Law.

Word order: frequency adverbs, auxiliaries

9 Put the words in parentheses in the correct places in the sentences, as in the example.

a I *sometimes* have dinner at my friend's house. (*sometimes*)

b Caroline eats fish. (*never*)

c I often eat in a restaurant. (*don't*)

d I get up late on a Sunday morning. (*usually*)

e It's very hot in August in my city. (*always*)

f The Brown family usually to Italy on vacation. (*go*)

g The weather always cold in January. (*is*)

h The bus is late. (*often*)

Vocabulary booster: everyday activities

10 **a)** Match the phrases from the box with the pictures below.

> brush your teeth ....   take a shower ....   go for a walk ....
> get dressed ....   wake up ....   go for a run .*a*.......
> catch a bus ....   go to the gym ....   cook a meal ....
> meet friends ....

b) 📼 Listen to the phrases on the recording. Practice saying them.

c) When do people usually do these things? Make a list.

in the morning	in the afternoon/evening
brush your teeth	*brush your teeth*
....	....
....	....
....	....
....	....
....	....

like, love, hate, + -ing

11 **a)** Read about Irene and Agnès and find out what they like and dislike about their life.

> Irene and Agnès are both au pairs: they live with a family, do housework (clean the house), and help with the children. In the afternoon, they go to an English class. in the evenings they often babysit (they stay at home with the children when their parents go out).

> 1 = *horrible!!! I hate it!* 2 = *don't like it* 3 = *OK* 4 = *I like it* 5 = *fantastic!!! I love it!!*

	Irene	Agnès
taking the children to school	2	4
doing housework	1	5
talking to the family	5	2
going to English class	4	1
babysitting	2	4

b) Write about their likes and dislikes.

1 (*taking the children to school*)
   Irene doesn't like taking the children to school.
   Agnès likes taking the children to school.

2 (*doing housework*)
   Irene ....
   Agnès ....

3 (*talking to the family*)
   Irene ....
   Agnès ....

4 (*going to English class*)
   Irene ....
   Agnès ....

5 (*babysitting*)
   Irene ....
   Agnès ....

Listen and read

12 **a)** 🔊 Read and listen to the text about English people's homes abroad.

"An Englishman's home," they say, "is his castle." Perhaps that's true ... but nowadays the home often isn't in England ... it's abroad!

More than half a million British people have a second home in another country. Many buy old houses in the south of France, or in Tuscany, in the north of Italy. The Eurostar train, which goes from London to Paris in three hours, makes it easy to go from one home to the other quickly. The Noteman family, who live in London, have a small house in Gascony. They sometimes go there for weekends, and they always spend the summer in France with their four children. Jerry Noteman says, " We really like living in France; the weather is usually good, we like the food and the wine, and the people are very friendly. We don't usually speak French when we go out ... most of our neighbors in the village are English, too!"

b) Answer these questions:

1 How many British people have a home abroad?
   More than half a million.

2 Where do they often buy houses?
   ....

3 Where does the Eurostar train go to?
   ....

4 Where do the Noteman family live in England?
   ....

5 Where do they live in France?
   ....

6 Where do they spend the summer?
   ....

7 How many children do they have?
   ....

8 What do they like about living in France?
   ....

9 Where do most of their neighbors come from?
   ....

Pronunciation

Plural nouns with /s/, /z/, and /ɪz/.

13 **a)** 🔊 Listen and notice the pronunciation of the plural form of these words.

book	books	/s/
key	keys	/z/
bus	buses	/ɪz/

b) Write the plural form of the nouns below. Do we pronounce the s at the end of the word as /s/, /z/, or /ɪz/?

1 dog*s*   .../z/...
2 crowd_   ....
3 spider_   ....
4 actress_   ....
5 beach_   ....
6 driver_   ....
7 student_   ....
8 restaurant_   ....
9 house_   ....
10 friend_   ....
11 parent_   ....
12 address_   ....

c) 🔊 Listen to the pronunciation of the words. Practice saying them.

Improve your writing

A paragraph about a friend

14 **a)** Match the questions and answers.

1 What's his name?   ....C....
2 Where does he come from?   ....
3 Where does he live now?   ....
4 What does he do?   ....
5 Where does he play?   ....
6 What does he like about life in London?   ....
7 What does he dislike about life in London?   ....
8 What does he think of the people?   ....

A He's a musician.
B In a bar called East and West.
C T̶a̶k̶a̶s̶h̶i̶.
D They're very nice when you know them.
E The rain.
F In London.
G Okinawa, in Japan.
H The international atmosphere.

b) Use the information to write a paragraph about Takashi, like this:

My friend Takashi .... Okinawa, in Japan, but now he .... in London.

.... a musician, and .... in a bar called East and West. He .... the international atmosphere in London, but .... the rain! He .... the people are very nice ....

module 5

can/can't

1 Look at the expressway signs. What can/can't you do on the expressway? Complete the sentences.

a You ....*can't*.......... stop on the expressway.

b You .... drive at 100 kilometers an hour.

c You .... drive at 180 kilometers an hour.

d You .... ride a bicycle on the expressway.

e You .... walk on the expressway.

f You .... find something to eat and drink at the service station.

g You .... buy gasoline at the service station.

h You .... turn around.

Short answers

2

> **Short answers with *can***
> LOOK!
>
> **Can** I/you/he/she/we/they drive?
>
> Yes, I/you/he/she/we/they **can**.
> No, I/you/he/she/we/they **can't**.

a) Write the short answers.

1 It's 8:30 in the morning. Can I park here? ....

2 Can I park here on a Sunday? ....

3 Can I smoke here? ....

4 Can I smoke here? ....

> **SORRY** No children under 18

5 Tom and Barbara are 16 years old. Can they go in? ....

6 I'm 19 years old. Can I go in? ....

> ☀ **WALK**

7 Can I cross the road now? ....

> **NO DOGS**

8 I've got a dog. Can it come in? ....

9 Excuse me, can we buy a phonecard here? ....

b) 💻 Listen to the questions and answers. Practice saying them.

28

Articles: *a* and *the*

3 Write *a* or *the* in the correct places in the sentences, as in the examples.

a Can you ride/bicycle? *(a)*

b Does it take/long time to get to/station? *(a) (the)*

c I always drive to work, but lot of people come by subway.

d Parking is real problem near my house.

e The traffic is very bad in evening.

f My uncle is train conductor.

g Do you have car?

h We live in small town in United States.

4 In each sentence, one *the* is unnecessary. Cross it out, as in the example.

a Parking is very difficult in the town, so I always go there by ~~the~~ bus.

b Eight o'clock is a good time to phone Thomas: he is always at the home in the evening.

c It's so cold today that a lot of people can't go to the work.

d The train times are different on the Sundays.

e What do you think of the public transportation in the London?

f You can use a rail pass in most countries in the Europe.

g Do the people drive on the left in the United States?

h Our plane arrives in Los Angeles at the two o'clock in the afternoon.

most, a lot of, some, not many

5 Rearrange the words to make sentences.

a a bicycle – children – learn – Most – to ride
  Most children learn to ride a bicycle.

b many – Not – on – people – Sundays – work

  ....

c on vacation – British people – A lot of – go to Spain

  ....

d can't – coffee – drink – without sugar – people – Some

  ....

e lot of – flying – like – people – A – don't

  ....

f Not many – understand – Japanese – European people – can

  ....

g enjoy – to tourists – Most – in my town – people – talking

  ....

h drive – night – at – Some – people – dangerously

  ....

29

Listen and read

6 a) 🔊 Listen to and read the text about transportation statistics.

Transportation Statistics

6 is the number of hours it takes to travel from London to New York by plane.

44 is the number of platforms at New York's Grand Central Terminal Station. Half a million people use the station every day.

209 kilometers an hour is the speed of the Spanish AVE train, which goes from the capital city Madrid to Seville, in the south of Spain, a distance of 470 km. The journey takes about two and a half hours.

567 is the number of passengers who can travel in a Boeing 747-400 airplane. It can fly for more than 12,000 kilometers without stopping. That's from London to Tokyo and back again.

9,297 kilometers is the distance of the Trans-Siberian railroad, which goes from Moscow to the town of Vladivostok in eastern Russia. The journey takes seven days.

60,000 is the number of taxis in Mexico City.

6,000,000 kilometers is the total length of all the roads in the United States.

43,000,000 is the number of people who travel through Heathrow Airport, near London, every year.

b) Answer the questions about the text.

1 How long does it take to travel from Madrid to Seville on the *AVE* train?
   Two and a half hours.

2 Where does the Trans-Siberian railroad begin?
   ....

3 How many people can travel on a Boeing 747-400 airplane?
   ....

4 Which country has 6,000,000 kilometers of road?
   ....

5 How many people pass through Heathrow Airport every year?
   ....

6 Which city has 60,000 taxis?
   ....

7 Which railroad station has 44 platforms?
   ....

8 How long does it take to fly from London to New York?
   ....

Prepositions

7 Complete the sentences with *by*, *to*, *on*, *off*, *for*, or *from*.

a Most people go to work ..*by*.................. car.

b It's not possible to drive to the beach: go .... foot.

c My journey .... work usually takes about 30 minutes.

d In Thailand, cars drive .... the left.

e You can fly .... Scotland direct from Paris.

f This is where you wait .... a bus to the railroad station.

g Please wait for people to get .... the bus before you get ....

h I never walk .... town: I always go .... bus.

i This bus goes .... the airport to downtown Washington.

j It's a good idea to walk .... work in the morning.

Vocabulary

Means of transportation

8 What are the missing letters?

a B U S

b M _ T _ R C _ C _ E

c S C _ _ T _ R

d B _ C _ C L _

e C _ R

f _ _ R P L _ N _

g S T _ E _ _ C _ R

h T R _ _ N

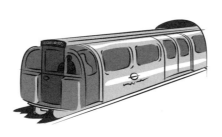

i _ U _ W A _

j T _ X _

Vocabulary booster: travel

9 **a)** Match the words from the box with the pictures.

> traffic light .... a bus stop .... a platform ....*1*....
> a crosswalk .... an expressway ....
> a ticket machine .... a railroad bridge .... a parking lot ....
> a sidewalk .... a parking meter ....

b) 🔊 Listen to the words. Practice saying them.

Pronunciation

The letter *a*

10 **a)** 🔊 We can pronounce the letter *a* in different ways.

/ɑː/	/eɪ/	/ɒː/	/æ/
father	make	walk	catch
....	....	....	..*can't*..
....	....	....	....
....	....	....	....

b) Write these words in the correct column above.

> ~~can't~~ taxi take small
> train cross talk
> comic travel wait fall

c) 🔊 Listen to the words. Practice saying them.

Spelling

11 Find **ten** spelling mistakes. <u>Underline</u> and correct them, as in the example.

traffic

Everybody knows that the/trafic in our city is really bad, and there are always traffic jams in the morning and evning. I don't have a car, so like most people, I usually travell by bus. My jorney home takes more than an hour. Also, the bus is very croded and sometimes I have to wait a long time for a bus wich isn't full.

If I rid my bicicle, it only takes therty minutes ... but it isn't easy because of all the cars on the strits.

Improve your writing

Completing an immigration form

12 Use the information below and complete Robert's immigration form.

AMERICAN Airways

YOUR FLIGHT DETAILS

For:	PRESTON / R MR.
Booking Ref:	GSKTFM
Date of Flight:	THURSDAY, OCTOBER 15, 01
From:	LIMA
To:	MIAMI
Airline:	AMERICAN AIRWAYS
Flight no:	AA 9295

PASSPORT

UNITED KINGDOM OF GREAT BRITAIN AND NORTHE

Name of bearer
Mr. Robert Alexander PRESTON

National Status
UK CITIZEN

No. of passport
737935 G

Place of Birth
Eastbourne, East Sussex

Date of Birth
12 February 1981

P<GBRPRESTON<<ROBERT<ALEXANDER<<
000050749066GBR810212M080212<<<<<<<<<<

VISA WAIVER   Immigration

Type or print legibly with pen in ALL CAPITAL LETTERS. **USE ENGLISH**.

1. Family name

2. First (given) name

3. Birth Date (*mo / day / yr*)

4. Country of Citizenship

5. Sex (*male or female*)

6. Passport Number

7. Airline and Flight Number

8. Country where you live

9. City where you boarded

CERTIFICATION: I certify that I have read and understand all the questions and statements on this form. The answers I have furnished are true and correct to the best of my knowledge and belief.

_____   _____
Signature   Date

module 6

Countable and uncountable nouns

1 a) Nine more of the words in the box are uncountable nouns. (Circle) them.

(butter) fruit meat water
tea journey cheese
hamburger egg vegetable
music bread food sugar
knife cookie

b) Underline the correct word or words, as in the example.

1 Check that the water *are*/<u>*is*</u> clean before you drink it.

2 The sugar *is*/*are* on the table.

3 The food in our hotel *aren't*/*isn't* very good. We eat all our *meal*/*meals* in a restaurant.

4 The journey from Miami to London *take*/*takes* about six hours.

5 Do you like *these*/*this* music? *It's*/*They're* by Mozart.

6 Everybody says that vegetables *are*/*is* very good for you.

7 It's not healthy to eat *too much*/*too many* hamburgers.

8 Fruit *isn't*/*aren't* expensive in my country.

Vocabulary

Food

2 In the box, find:

Drinks	Types of fruit	Other things you can eat	
mineral water	*banana*	....	....
....	....	....	....
....	....	....	....
....	....	....	....
....	....	....	

J	O	J	E	L	L	Y	N	N	S	C	E
B	F	A	S	B	U	T	T	E	R	O	T
B	R	E	A	D	I	E	A	O	N	F	B
N	U	T	S	G	B	A	A	R	C	F	H
M	I	N	E	R	A	L	W	A	T	E	R
P	T	A	A	A	N	P	I	N	R	E	Y
T	J	P	I	P	A	I	C	G	C	T	O
A	U	P	N	E	N	Z	E	E	H	U	G
M	I	L	K	S	A	Z	M	M	E	E	U
R	C	E	G	G	S	A	E	H	E	I	R
C	E	R	E	A	L	T	O	A	S	T	T
S	A	U	S	A	G	E	S	M	E	N	T

there is/there are

3 Complete the sentences with the correct form of *there is/there are*.

a *Is there* .... any milk in the fridge?

b How many students .... in your class?

c .... a very good beach near our hotel.

d .... any cheap restaurants near here?

e .... a university in Brighton?

f I'm sorry, but .... any stores open at this time.

g .... fifty states in the US.

h .... any milk. How about lemon in your tea?

i .... a computer room in the school?

j .... three big parks in the city.

Short answers

4 **a)** Read the information about two campsites: *Les Pins* and *Las Molinas*.

Les Pins	Las Molinas
Five minutes' walk to the beach	Beautiful mountain location
Tennis courts	Swimming pool
Restaurant, drinks bar	Bar
Children's playground	Supermarket, souvenir store
Stores, etc. in village of Choisy (5 km)	10 km from the historic town of Los Pozos (stores, restaurants, bars, etc.)

Short answers with *there is* and *there are* **LOOK!**

Is there a hotel near here? Yes, **there is**.
No, **there isn't**.

Are there any good restaurants? Yes, **there are**.
No, **there aren't**.

---

b) Complete the questions, and write the correct short answer.

at Les Pins:

1 *Is*............ there a beach?
   Yes, there is. ....

2 .... there any places to eat and drink?
   ....

3 .... there a swimming pool?
   ....

4 .... there a children's playground?
   ....

5 .... there a supermarket?
   ....

at Las Molinas:

6 .... there a beach?
   No, there isn't. ....

7 .... there a restaurant?
   ....

8 .... there any tennis courts?
   ....

9 .... a bar?
   ....

10 .... there any stores?
   ....

11 .... there any interesting towns to visit?
   ....

c) 📼 Listen to the sentences on the recording. Practice saying them.

some and *any*

5 a) Complete the sentences with *some* or *any*.

1 No, thanks, I don't drink coffee ... do you have ...*any*........ orange juice?

2 There are .... messages for you on the answering machine.

3 There's .... salt on the table, but there isn't .... pepper.

4 We can't make an omelet because we don't have .... eggs.

5 Would you like .... milk in your coffee?

6 There's .... butter on the table.

7 Sorry, we don't have .... more bread. Would you like .... crackers with your cheese?

8 I'm sorry, we don't have .... hot food, but we've got .... sandwiches if you're hungry.

b) 💬 Listen to the sentences on the recording. Practice saying them.

some, any, a(n), and *no*

6 a) Helen and Carlos want to buy a sandwich for their lunch. Complete the conversation in the sandwich store with *some*, *any*, *a(n)*, or *no*.

SALES CLERK: Yes, what would you like?

HELEN: Let me see ... I'd like (1) ...*an*........ egg sandwich, please.

SALES CLERK: OK, one egg sandwich ... butter?

HELEN: No, thanks, (2) .... butter. I'm on (3) .... diet.

SALES CLERK: OK ... here you are. Anything else with that? We have (4) .... very nice fruit ... bananas, apples ...

HELEN: Yes. (5) .... apple, please.

SALES CLERK: OK, that's $2.50. And for you, sir?

CARLOS: Hmm. Do you have (6) .... Swiss cheese?

SALES CLERK: No, sorry. There's (7) .... Swiss cheese, but we have (8) .... very good Cheddar ... it's English cheese, it's very good.

CARLOS: OK. (9) .... Cheddar cheese sandwich, please. Can I have (10) .... salad with that?

SALES CLERK: Sure. Would you like (11) .... drink?

HELEN: Yes, (12) .... bottle of mineral water, please.

b) 💬 Listen to the conversation. Practice saying it.

Vocabulary booster: things to eat

7 **a)** Label the pictures with words from the box.

> rice   potato chips   potatoes   salt   salad   oil
> olives   tomatoes   pepper   onions   French fries
> vinegar

1 rice

7

2

8

3

9

4

10

5

11

6

12

b) 📼 Listen to the pronunciation of the words.

Listen and read

8 📼 Read and listen to the recipe. Check (✓) the correct picture.

Ⓐ    Ⓑ

Ⓒ    Ⓓ

——— Fish Cakes ———

Ingredients (to make 24 fish cakes):

> 500g boiled potatoes
> 350g cooked white fish
> 1 tablespoon tomato purée
> 2 tablespoons mixed herbs
> 50g breadcrumbs
> a little oil
> salt and pepper

Method:

1 Mash the boiled potatoes with a little salt and pepper.
2 Mix together the potatoes and the fish, tomato purée, and herbs.
3 Add a little salt and pepper.
4 Make 24 fish cakes from the mixture. Cover the fish cakes with the breadcrumbs.
5 Heat the oil in a frying pan. Fry the fish cakes for about five minutes, turning them once.
6 Serve the fish cakes immediately with tomato sauce and a salad.

Questions with *how much* and *how many*

9 Complete these questions about the recipe on page 37, using *how much* or *how many*.

a ..*How many*.. fish cakes does this recipe make?

– Twenty-four.

b .... fish do you need?

– 350g.

c .... potato do you use in the recipe?

– 500g.

d .... tablespoons of herbs do you need?

– Two.

e .... tomato purée do you add?

– 1 tablespoon.

f .... oil do you use?

– A little.

g .... grams of breadcrumbs do you need?

– 50.

h .... minutes do you cook the fishcakes?

– About five.

Vocabulary

Containers: *a cup of*, *a glass of*, *a bottle of*

10 a) Label the pictures with words from the box.

| a bag | a bottle | a carton | ~~a cup~~ | a glass | a pack |

1 *a cup*........

2 ....

3 ....

4 ....

5 ....

6 ....

b) Complete the phrases with a suitable word from the box above (sometimes more than one answer is possible).

1 a ..*bottle*.. of mineral water
2 a .... of cigarettes
3 a .... of milk
4 a .... of sugar
5 a .... of cookies
6 a .... of lemonade
7 a .... of coffee
8 a .... of water
9 a .... of orange juice
10 a .... of tea

Pronunciation

Sentence stress

11 a) 🖵 Listen to the recording. <u>Underline</u> the words which have the main sentence stress, as in the example.

1 Can I have a <u>bottle</u> of <u>mineral</u> water, <u>please</u>?

2 You can catch a bus to the airport from here.

3 How many packs of cigarettes do you buy in a week?

4 How much money do you <u>have</u> in your bag?

5 I always have orange juice with my breakfast.

6 How much water do you drink in a day?

7 What do you want for lunch?

8 I never drink coffee in the evening.

b) 🖵 Listen again and practice saying the sentences.

Improve your writing

Describing food from your country

12 **a)** What nationality is the writer of each paragraph? Choose from the words in the box.

| Italian | Mexican | Argentinian | Japanese | French | Hungarian | Spanish |

1 .... 2 .... 3 .... 4 .... 5 ....

① Pizza is a very famous food from my country. Originally it comes from Naples, in the south of my country. A traditional pizza has cheese - mozzarella cheese - tomato and herbs. A lot of young people go to a pizza restaurant on Sunday evenings.
Andrea

② People don't use a knife and fork to eat the traditional food of my country: we use wooden sticks called chopsticks. Sushi is a very famous dish with fish, rice, and sometimes vegetables.
Kaori

③ A typical breakfast in my country is a very big cup of strong coffee, with lots of milk. The traditional thing to eat with your coffee is a croissant, maybe with butter or jam.
Jean-Christophe

④ People eat a lot of meat in my country, especially beef. On Sundays, people have a traditional lunch called an asado. In my family, my father cooks the meat on a barbecue, and we eat it with lots of salad.
Oscar

⑤ The national dish of my country is gulyásleves. Many people think it's a meat dish but if you have real gulyás, it's a soup with lots of meat and vegetables.
Eva

b) Write a few sentences about food in your country. Use some of these phrases to help you.

Useful Language

... is a very famous food from my country.

Originally it comes from ... in the south/north of my country.

The national dish of my country is ... .

... is a famous dish with ... and ... .

A typical breakfast in my country is ... .

The traditional thing to eat with ... is ... .

People eat a lot of ... in my country.

On Sunday, many people have ... for lunch.

We eat it with lots of ... .

module 7

Past Simple: *was/were*

1 Complete the sentences with *was* or *were*.

a My grandparents ....*were*.... married for more than fifty years.

b When I .... in Berlin last year, the weather .... very cold.

c How many people .... there at the party?

d Where .... you on Saturday evening?

e It .... a beautiful day in August. My family and I .... on vacation at the seaside.

f .... George at school today?

g How .... your first day at work?

h It .... very nice to meet you, Mr Brown.

Short answers

2 a) Read about the famous people. Complete the questions and the short answers.

Mark Twain
American writer
– born 1835 –
died 1910

1 .*Was*........ Mark Twain a painter?
.*No, he wasn't.*

2 .*Was*........ he American?
.*Yes, he was.*

Charlie Chaplin
Film actor – born
London 1889 – died
Switzerland 1977

3 .... Charlie Chaplin born in America?

....

4 .... he an actor?

....

The Marx Brothers
American comedians –
all born in Germany

5 .... the Marx Brothers born in the US?

....

6 .... they comedians?

....

Anna Pavlova
Russian dancer –
died 1931

7 .... Anna Pavlova Russian?

....

8 .... she a singer?

....

b) 📼 Listen to the recording. Practice saying the questions and answers.

Past Simple

Spelling of -ed endings.

3 Write the Past Simple tense of the verbs below.

a like _liked_

b enjoy ....

c travel ....

d study ....

e look ....

f dance ....

g play ....

h believe ....

i arrive ....

j try ....

k receive ....

l stay ....

Regular verbs

4 Complete the sentences in the Past Simple. Use a verb from the box below.

> ~~graduate~~ study change try start die
> end live help walk

a My brother was a student at Glasgow University: He _graduated_ last year.

b World War II .... in 1939, and .... six years later, in 1945.

c Elvis Presley – The King of Rock 'n' Roll – .... in 1977.

d There were no more buses, so I .... home.

e When I was in school, my parents often .... me with my homework.

f I .... French when I was in school, but I don't remember very much now.

g I .... to phone you last night, but there was no answer.

h When he was a young musician, Reg Dwight .... his name to Elton John.

i The composer Chopin was born in Poland, but he .... in France for many years.

Irregular verbs

5 Complete the sentences with the past forms of the verbs in parentheses.

Three Child Stars of the Past

Mozart ...

a _wrote_ music when he was five years old; (*write*)

b .... home when he was only twelve years old; (*leave*)

c .... to live in Vienna when he was 25 years old. (*go*)

Wolfgang Amadeus Mozart – composer

Donny Osmond ...

d .... singing on television at the age of five; (*begin*)

e .... with his five brothers in the Osmond Brothers; (*sing*)

f .... millions of records before he was 18. (*sell*)

Donny Osmond – pop star

Shirley Temple ...

g .... her first movie when she was six; (*make*)

h .... an Oscar in 1934; (*win*)

i .... a politician in the 1970s. (*become*)

Shirley Temple – actress

Regular and irregular verbs

6 **a)** Complete this text about Amelia Earhart, using the correct form of the verbs.

Seventy years ago, Amelia Earhart (1) ..*was*.. (*be*) America's favorite woman. In 1932, she (2) .... (*fly*) across the Atlantic Ocean alone: the first woman to do this. Her journey (3) .... (*start*) in Newfoundland, Canada: fifteen hours later, her Lockheed Vega airplane (4) .... (*arrive*) in Londonderry, Ireland. People all over the world (5) .... (*want*) to meet this incredible woman. She (6) .... (*meet*) King George V of England and (7) .... (*become*) friends with the US President, Franklin D. Roosevelt. The American people (8) .... (*love*) her.

Five years later, Amelia (9) .... (*try*) to fly around the world. An American university (10) .... (*give*) her $50,000 for a new Lockheed Electra airplane. On the morning of July 2nd, 1937, Amelia and her copilot, Fred Noonan (11) .... (*leave*) Lae, in New Guinea, and (12) .... (*begin*) their journey to Howland Island in the Pacific Ocean.

On July 3rd, 1937, the American ship *Itasca* (13) .... (*receive*) a radio message from Amelia: a few minutes later her plane (14) .... (*disappear*). American ships (15) .... (*spend*) nearly two weeks looking for the plane, but they (16) .... (*find*) nothing.

b) 📟 Listen and check your answers.

Past time phrases

7 <u>Underline</u> the correct time phrase to complete each sentence.

a Disco music was very popular *nowadays/<u>in the 1970s</u>*.

b People started traveling by train *in the nineteenth century/in the twenty-first century*.

c People usually go to college *when they are 18/when they were 18*.

d My family lived in the United States *now/when I was a child*.

e Yugoslavia was world basketball champion *in 1990/now*.

f I go to the swimming pool *every week/last week*.

g I visited my friends in Canada *three years ago/every year*.

Prepositions of time

8 Complete the sentences with *at, from, in, on,* or *to.*

a The economic situation in our country became much better ...*in*.......... the 1990s.

b The coffee shop is open .... eight-thirty in the morning .... about eleven o'clock in the evening.

c We arrived at the hotel .... about eleven o'clock.

d We decided to have our vacation .... September, when it's not so hot.

e .... the age of seven, Vanessa started dancing lessons.

f I stayed at home .... Friday because I had so much work to do.

g "When were you born?"
"............... 1986."

h There was a war between the two countries .... the nineteenth century.

Pronunciation

Past tense endings

9 **a)** Look at the past forms below. Is the pronunciation of the <u>underlined</u> sounds the same (S) or different (D)?

1	b<u>ou</u>ght	c<u>au</u>ght	.S.......
2	wr<u>o</u>te	c<u>o</u>st	.D.......
3	s<u>ai</u>d	r<u>ea</u>d	....
4	p<u>u</u>t	c<u>u</u>t	....
5	s<u>aw</u>	f<u>ou</u>nd	....
6	c<u>a</u>me	g<u>a</u>ve	....
7	l<u>o</u>st	c<u>o</u>st	....
8	t<u>oo</u>k	st<u>oo</u>d	....
9	w<u>o</u>re	c<u>au</u>ght	....
10	h<u>ea</u>rd	w<u>o</u>n	....

b) 📼 Listen to the recording. Practice saying the words. Copy the voice.

Vocabulary booster: common verbs

10 **a)** Label the pictures with the words from the box.

~~break~~	build	catch	cut	fall	run	steal
throw	wake up	win				

b) Here are the past forms of the verbs in the box. Write the infinitive form next to the past form.

1	broke	*break*...	6	ran	....
2	caught	....	7	stole	....
3	built	....	8	fell	....
4	threw	....	9	cut	....
5	woke up	....	10	won	....

c) 📼 Listen to the pronunciation of the infinitive and past forms. Practice saying them, copying the voices on the recording.

Listen and read

11 **a)** 📼 Read and listen to the story of *The Strange Soldier*.

The Strange Soldier

It was a beautiful sunny morning in Mexico City. The date was October 10th, the year was 1593.

In the main square of the city, soldiers stood in front of the Royal Palace. The people of the city came and went as usual. But there was something strange about one of the soldiers: he wore a different uniform from the others, and had a different type of gun. When the other soldiers saw him, they began asking him questions. "Who are you? Where are you from?" one of the other soldiers asked. "I am a Spanish soldier," he answered "and because the governor died last night, it is my job to stay in front of the palace here." "The governor?" one of the soldiers replied. "Which governor?" "The governor of Manila, of course."
The other soldiers told him he was in Mexico City – thousands of kilometers from the city of Manila.
The young soldier was amazed and had no idea how he came to be in a city so far from his home. Nobody believed his strange story. In the end, they put the young man in prison, and left him there until they decided what to do.

Two months later, a Spanish ship arrived from Manila. It brought news that the governor of Manila was dead – and the time of his death was 10 p.m. on the evening of October 9th, 1593. Was the young man's story true?

Four hundred years later, no one knows how it was possible for a man to travel across the world in one night ... without knowing how or why.

b) Read the story again. Put these events in the order they happened.

A The Mexican soldiers saw the strange

soldier. ....

B The governor of Manila died. ....*1*....

C They put the strange soldier in prison. ....

D A ship from Manila arrived in

Mexico City. ....

E The strange soldier traveled from

Manila to Mexico. ....

Ordinal numbers

12 Write an ordinal number to complete the sentences. Use the numbers to help you.

a Ronald Reagan was the .*fortieth*........

President of the United States. (*40*)

b "What's the .... month in the year?" (*5*)

"May."

c Our apartment is on the .... floor. (*8*)

d Beethoven wrote his music in the ....

century. (*19*)

e Brazil won the World Cup for the ....

time in 1994. (*4*)

f The Berlin Wall fell near the end of the

.... century. (*20*)

g Neil Armstrong was the .... man on

the moon, and Buzz Aldrin was the

.... (*1/2*)

h My sister's birthday is on August ....

(*22*)

Improve your writing

13 Time linkers: *before*, *after*, *then*

Before I went to bed, I phoned Suzanne.
I phoned Suzanne **before** I went to bed.

After Jane left college, she traveled to India.
Jane traveled to India **after** she left college.

Sebastian was a waiter in a restaurant.
Then he found another job.

Join the sentences below with *before*, *after*, or *then*.

a .*Before*.......... I went home, I bought something

to eat from the supermarket.

b .... their dog died, the house was very

quiet.

c We had time for a cup of coffee ....

the train left.

d In the morning, I went shopping with my

friend Sara. .... we had lunch.

e For a long time, nobody spoke. ....

someone asked a question.

f .... they got married, Paul and Linda

usually stayed at home on Saturday nights.

g .... he was a famous actor, Bruce

worked as a taxi driver.

h I remembered to close all the windows

.... I went out.

module 8

Vocabulary

Common verbs in the past tense

1 Complete the sentences with the past tense of the verbs in parentheses.

a Chris was so hungry he
.ate.............. (eat) three burgers
and two plates of French fries!

b We went shopping on Saturday –
I .... (buy) a new skirt.

c I .... (read) *Alice in
Wonderland* when I was seven
years old.

d It was a very long journey, but I
.... (sleep) on the train
for a few hours.

e I .... (see) my cousin in
the park.

f It was a beautiful day on
Sunday, so we .... (drive)
to the country and had a picnic.

g Do you know who ....
(write) *Don Quijote* ?

h I'm sorry I'm late ... when I
.... (wake up) it was
nearly ten o'clock!

i Is it true that Robin Hood always
.... (wear) green?

j The police looked everywhere for
the money, but they only
.... (find) an empty bag.

k Lucy's parents .... (give)
her a car for her 21st birthday.

l We were so hot and thirsty that
we both .... (drink) a
liter bottle of mineral water.

m It was a very boring concert.
Some people .... (fall)
asleep.

Past Simple

Negative

2 Make the sentences below negative.

a We had good weather when we were on vacation.
We didn't have good weather when we were on vacation.

b We went for a drive yesterday.
....

c Ben remembered to buy a birthday card.
....

d I heard the telephone.
....

e The letter arrived this morning.
....

f I ate in a restaurant last night.
....

g Amanda knew what to do.
....

h I checked my email yesterday.
....

Questions

3 Write questions about these famous people from the past.

a Shakespeare/write/*Romeo and Juliet*
Did Shakespeare write "Romeo and Juliet"?

b Alexander Graham Bell/invent/email
....

c Marilyn Monroe/sing/"Candle in the Wind"
....

d Captain Cook/discover/America
....

e Leonardo da Vinci/paint/the *Mona Lisa*
....

f Madonna/play/Evita
....

g Beethoven/write/rock songs

....

h Laurel and Hardy/make/comedy movies

....

i Yuri Gagarin/travel/to the moon

....

Short answers

4

> **Short answers with the Past Simple** LOOK!
>
> **Did** I/you/he/she/it/we/they know?
>
> **Yes**, I/you/he/she/it/we/they **did**.
> **No**, I/you/he/she/it/we/they **didn't**.

a) Look again at the questions in exercise 3.
Write the correct short answer for each question.

1 *Yes, he did.* ....
2 ....
3 ....
4 ....
5 ....
6 ....
7 ....
8 ....
9 ....

b) 📼 Listen to the questions and answers on
the recording. Practice saying them.

Question words

5 **a)** A few days ago, Simon went on a
business trip. Look at the papers in his
wallet, and write questions about his day.

Eurolink

London - Paris	(ONE-WAY)
Departure time	14:30
Journey time	3 HOURS

```
The Station Buffet Restaurant

     1 set menu              £14.50
     + SERVICE (10%)
```

The Station Bookstore

| Blue Guide to France | 9.99 |
| English–French Dictionary | 4.99 |

Total £15.95

BUREAU DE CHANGE

£200 changed to French francs

1 *Where did he* .... go?

He went to Paris.

2 .... travel?

By train.

3 .... have lunch?

At The Station Buffet Restaurant.

4 .... cost?

£15.95.

5 .... at the station?

Some books.

6 .... buy?

Two.

7 .... change?

£200.

8 .... leave?

At 14:30.

9 .... take?

Three hours.

b) 📼 Listen to the questions and answers on
the recording. Practice saying them.

Past Simple

Positive, negative, and question forms

6 Underline the word that is **incorrect** in the following sentences. Write in the correct word.

a Did you <u>had</u>/a nice *have* weekend?

b Did you see Jan at the party? – Yes, I saw.

c I'm sorry, what did you said?

d What time did you got up this morning?

e It was a very long flight: the journey take more than thirteen hours.

f We went to the shopping center yesterday, but we didn't bought anything.

g I come home early because I felt very tired.

h Did you enjoyed the movie?

i I didn't understood what they said to me.

j Where did you went on Friday night?

Prepositions

7 Complete the sentences with the correct preposition from the box.

| up | ~~at~~ | in | by | to | out | in | about |

a I looked ..*at*.......... my watch: it was nearly ten o'clock.

b Linda woke .... at nine o'clock.

c The story is that Robin Hood gave all his money .... poor people.

d Michael and Kate fell .... love when they were in college.

e The Prince lived .... an old castle in the mountains.

f I had a lot of work to do on Sunday, so I didn't go ....

g The author Jane Wilson wrote a book .... her journey to Africa.

h How did you travel to Mexico? – We went .... plane.

Pronunciation

Past forms

8 **a)** 🖭 Listen to the pronunciation of the past forms on the recording. Notice how the pronunciation of the sound **in bold** is the same.

/æ/	had	began	.*ran*...............	....
/e/	read	fell	....	....
/ɒː/	caught	bought	....	....
/ʌ/	cut	shut	....	....

b) What is the past form of the verbs in the box? Put them in one of the above groups according to the pronunciation of the past form.

| leave | meet | ~~run~~ | see | think | win |

c) 🖭 Listen to the pronunciation of words on the recording. Practice saying them.

Vocabulary booster: books, magazines, and newspapers

9 **a)** Label the pictures with the words from the box.

> headline   article   front page
> ~~newspaper~~   ~~magazine~~   picture
> advertisement   pages   cover   title
> author   ~~book~~

1   *newspaper*

2   ....

3   ....

4   ....

5   *magazine*

6   ....

7   ....

8   ....

9   *book*

10   ....

11   ....

12   ....

DAILY NEWS
Newspaper of the Year
JANUARY 25th, 2001   www.daily.news.co.uk

WOMAN WITH A MISSION
BOB JOHNSON'S NATIONWIDE QUEST FOR FEMALE FINANCIAL ADVICE

New sales blow hits Superstores

Poor Christmas profits deepen gloom for Superstore

By Tom Barley

INSIDE: JERRY WILSON 4-5 • SHOPPING 11 • SHARES & MARKET PRICES 12-13

The Image

WHAT'S **HOT** THIS SUMMER

Now the nights are getting lighter, it's time to turn on the heat. No problem – just grab a brush and comb, and style you hair to these ten styles...

YOUR LETTERS

FASHION NEWS FROM NEW YORK

Now! *Silver Shine* Nail Varnish

page 12

TREASURE ISLAND
ROBERT LOUIS STEVENSON

b) 🎧 Listen to the pronunciation of the words on the recording. Practice saying them.

Listen and read

10 **a)** 🔊 Read and listen to the text about the three heroes/heroines.

National heroes and heroines

John Sobieski (King John III)

John Sobieski is an important national hero in Poland. He was born in 1624. He became King of Poland at the age of fifty, and he fought many <u>battles</u> against the Turks, who at that time controlled a large part of Central and Eastern Europe. In 1683, he became the hero of the Christian world when he won a great victory at Vienna, in what is now Austria. It was an important moment in the history of Europe. John Sobieski died in 1696.

Florence Nightingale

A hundred and fifty years ago, most nurses did not study nursing, but a British woman called Florence Nightingale tried to change all that. In the 1850s, she worked in a hospital for <u>wounded</u> soldiers in the Crimea (now Ukraine). People say she never slept, but spent all her time helping the men. The soldiers called her "The Lady of the Lamp" because of the lamp she always carried as she walked around at night. When she returned to England, she began a school of nursing in London. She died in 1910.

Che Guevara

A hero for some – and for others, a <u>villain</u> – his real name was Ernesto Guevara de la Serna, and he was born in Rosario, Argentina, in 1928. He studied to be a doctor in Buenos Aires, but became interested in politics as a young man. He spent time in Guatemala and Mexico and was a government minister in Cuba in the 1960s. He died in Bolivia in 1967 when he tried to start a revolution against the military government. He later became a hero for many young people in the 1960s and 70s because of his good looks and his revolutionary political ideas.

Glossary   *battle* = a fight between soldiers   *wounded* = hurt in a battle or war
villain = a bad person, a criminal

b) Write the questions for the answers, as in the example.

1 *When was John Sobieski born?*

In 1624.

2 ....

....

When he was fifty years old.

3 ....

....

Because he won a great victory at Vienna.

4 ....

....

In 1696.

5 ....

....

In the 1850s.

6 ....

....

"The Lady of the Lamp."

7 ....

....

When she returned to England.

8 ....

....

In Buenos Aires.

9 ....

....

When he was a young man.

10 ....

....

Because of his good looks and revolutionary political ideas.

Improve your writing

A diary

11 **a)** Ray is a young Australian on vacation in Europe. He decided to travel from London to Prague by bus. Read his vacation diary and put the phrases below in the best place.

a ~~in the evening~~	b I didn't have any euros
c the bus wasn't there	d and listened to the music
e only cost £50	f we finally left London
g When we arrived in France	h I walked back to the parking lot
i was in another country	

Sunday

Today was my last day in London. I spent the afternoon walking around, and (1) ......a...... I met two of my friends in a place called the Southern Lights, near Victoria Station. We talked (2) ....
I felt sorry to leave London, but everybody says Prague is a really beautiful city. I went home early – about ten o'clock – and packed my suitcase for tomorrow. London to Prague is 22 hours on the bus – it's a long journey, but my ticket (3) ....

Monday

We left Victoria Coach Station at about 1 o'clock. The bus was full of people, mostly young. There were one or two Australians and a lot of other nationalities too! The traffic was really bad at that time and it was nearly an hour before (4) ....
We arrived in Dover in the afternoon and took the ferry across the English Channel. (5) .... they asked to see my passport ... and then they told me I needed to pay for a visa!!

Tuesday

I fell asleep somewhere in the north of France ... I felt so tired and when I woke up I (6) .... !!
The expressway was full of big German cars and everybody drove at about 150 kph!! About ten o'clock, we stopped at a gas station, and I went into the store for something to eat and drink. Then I remembered (7) .... to pay for it. In the end, a very kind person changed my $ US into euros for me, and I bought something to eat and drink. Twenty minutes later, (8) .... Life was good: I had food, drink, and it was only four more hours to Prague. There was only one problem ... (9) .... !!

b) Complete Ray's diary with words from the box.

~~were~~	drove	opened	sat	spoke	thought
got	stopped	helped	saw	started	said
remembered	told	~~was~~			

I was in a complete panic. My bag, my clothes, and my passport (1) .were....... all on the bus, the bus (2) .was........ on the expressway ... and I was at the gas station. I (3) .... down by the road, thinking, "What can I do? Help!!"
And soon someone (4) .... me. A kind German woman – who (5) .... perfect English – asked me if there was a problem. I (6) .... her about the bus, and she (7) .... she could help me.
We (8) .... into her big German car – it was a Mercedes – and we (9) .... along the expressway at about 180 kilometers an hour. A few minutes later, we (10) .... the bus – my bus. My new German friend (11) .... her window and (12) .... shouting "Stop!! Stop!!" at the bus driver (in German, of course!!). At first, the bus driver (13) .... she was crazy and drove faster ... until he saw me. Perhaps he (14) .... my face. Then we drove along together until the next expressway gas station, and then we both (15) ....

module 9

Adjectives: opposites

1 Write the opposite of:

a an expensive hotel
   a cheap hotel

b a difficult question

   ....

c a big country

   ....

d an attractive face

   ....

e an old bicycle

   ....

f a comfortable chair

   ....

g a slow train

   ....

Comparative adjectives

2 Add the correct letters to make the comparative form of the adjectives below.

a young *e r*

b eas _ _ _

c big _ _ _

d cheap _ _

e health _ _ _

f new _ _

g happ _ _ _

h slim _ _ _

i quiet _ _

j hot _ _ _

3 a) Read the two facts, then write a sentence using the comparative form of the adjective.

1 The area of Brazil is 8.5 million km^2
   The area of Australia is 7.6 million km^2
   Brazil is bigger than Australia. ....
   .... (*big*)

2 The Volga River in Russia is 3,500 km long.
   The Mississippi River in the US is 6,000 km long.
   ....
   .... (*long*)

3 Blue whales usually weigh about 130 tons.
   Elephants usually weigh about 7 tons.
   ....
   .... (*heavy*)

4 The Pyramids in Egypt are about 4,000 years old.
   The Parthenon in Greece is about 2,500 years old.
   ....
   .... (*old*)

5 The Sears Tower in Chicago is 443 m tall.
   The Empire State building, New York, is 381 m tall.
   ....
   .... (*tall*)

6 The Akashi–Kaikyo Bridge in Japan is nearly 2,000 m long.
   The Sydney Harbour Bridge in Australia is 500 m long.
   ....
   .... (*long*)

7 The price of gold is about $8,000 per kilo.
   The price of silver is about $150 per kilo.
   ....
   .... (*expensive*)

8 English has more than a hundred irregular verbs.
   Esperanto has no irregular verbs!
   ....
   .... (*easy*)

b) 🔊 Listen to the sentences on the recording and practice saying them.

Superlative adjectives

4 **a)** Read the information about the Olympic athletes below.

Roy Seagrove –

Rower

Age: 38
Height: 1 m 90
Weight: 95 kg
These are his fifth
Olympic Games
Three Olympic
medals up to now

Jim Bowen –

Basketball player

Age: 19
Height: 1 m 95
Weight: 89 kg
First Olympic Games
Started playing
basketball three
months ago

Lilian Kay –

Marathon runner

Age: 25
Height: 1 m 60
Weight: 51 kg
Silver medal in the
last Olympics

Karina Green –

Swimmer

Age: 16
Height: 1 m 72
Weight: 57 kg
First Olympic Games

b) Complete the sentences as in the example.

1 _Roy Seagrove_ is _the oldest_ . (*old*)
2 .... is .... (*young*)
3 .... has .... hair. (*long*)
4 .... has .... hair. (*short*)
5 .... is .... (*tall*)
6 .... is .... (*heavy*)
7 .... is .... (*small*)
8 .... is .... (*successful*)

5 Change the adjective into the superlative form. Can you answer the questions?

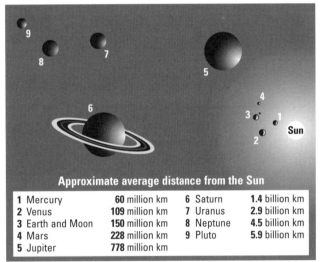

Approximate average distance from the Sun

1 Mercury	**60** million km	**6** Saturn	**1.4** billion km
2 Venus	**109** million km	**7** Uranus	**2.9** billion km
3 Earth and Moon	**150** million km	**8** Neptune	**4.5** billion km
4 Mars	**228** million km	**9** Pluto	**5.9** billion km
5 Jupiter	**778** million km		

a Which is _the nearest_ (*near*)
  planet to the Sun?   _Mercury_

b What's the name of
  .... (*small*) planet?   ....

c It has sixteen moons and it's
  .... (*big*) planet in
  the solar system.   ....

d Which is ....
  (*hot*) planet?   ....

e This is the .... (*far*)
  planet from the Sun, and also
  .... (*cold*).   ....

f Which planet is
  .... (*easy*)
  to see from the Earth?   ....

g Which planet is
  .... (*close*) to Earth? ....

Comparative and superlative adjectives

6 a) Complete the joke with the comparative or superlative forms of the adjectives.

A woman went into
(1) _the most expensive_ (expensive) butcher's in town and asked for (2) .... (big) chicken in the store. The storekeeper showed her a chicken and said, "This is (3) .... (good) chicken in the store, madam." "It's very small," she said. "Do you have a (4) .... (large) one?" "Just a moment," said the storekeeper. He took the chicken into another room. In fact it was the only chicken he had. So he put some sausages inside to make it look (5) .... (big). "Here you are," he said. "This is our (6) .... (delicious) chicken. And you can see that it's (7) .... (big) than the other. But I'm afraid it's also (8) .... (expensive)."
"Hmm ... but I'm not sure if it's (9) .... (good) than the other. OK. Can I have both of them, please?"

b) 🖭 Listen to the joke on the recording.

Vocabulary

Stores and shopping

7 a) Rearrange the letters to make the names of stores.

1 You buy steak at a
butcher's ......   B R U S H T E C

2 You buy shirts,
pants and skirts at a
....   L O S H C E T   R T S O E

3 You buy newspapers,
magazines, and cigarettes
at a
....   S W E D R N S E L A E

4 You buy things in
the open air at a
....   T R E S T E   T R A M E K

5 You buy books at a
....   K O S T E R O O B

6 You buy bread at a
....   S K E R A B

7 You buy ham and
cheese at a
....   E T G C Y R O S R R E O

8 You can buy stamps
and send parcels at a
....   S T O P   C O F F E I

9 You can buy medicine
at a
....   U G D T R S E R O

10 You can buy almost
everything at a
....   S U E T K R A M P E R

b) 🖭 Listen to the sentences on the recording. Practice saying them.

Pronunciation

Comparatives

8 a) 🔊 **Listen to the pronunciation of the adjectives below. Practice saying them.**

big   old
fast   expensive
slow   difficult

b) 🔊 **Listen to the comparative forms. Notice the pronunciation of *than*. Practice saying them.**

bigger than   older than
faster than   more expensive than
slower than   more difficult than

c) 🔊 **Listen to the sentences. Check (✔) the true ones and cross (✗) the false ones.**

1   Cats are bigger than tigers.
2   Trains are faster than airplanes.
3   Bicycles are slower than motorbikes.
4   New York is older than Rome.
5   Gold is more expensive than silver.
6   Driving a car is more difficult than riding a bicycle.

One and *ones*

9 Rewrite the sentences. Change the words in bold to *one* or *ones*.

a   I don't have my old car now. I bought a new **car** last week.

I bought a new *one last week* .

b   Martha has three children. The youngest **child** is nearly three.

The youngest ....

c   Your shoes are much more expensive than the **shoes** I bought.

Your shoes are much more expensive than

....

d   "Which color pen would you like?"

"The red **pen**, please."

The red ....

e   There are many old buildings downtown. These **buildings** are the oldest.

These ....

Improve your writing

Describing a place

10 a) **Complete this paragraph about *My Favorite Store* with phrases from the box.**

it sells   is open   The best time to go is ~~My favorite store is~~   until eight o'clock at night The reason I like it is   The people there

My Favorite Store

(1) *My favorite store is* called Talad Thai. It's in Putney, in south London. It's next to a Chinese restaurant, and (2) .... all kinds of food from China, Thailand, and many other countries in the Far East.

(3) .... because I love cooking, especially Oriental food. The store (4) .... seven days a week, from ten o'clock in the morning (5) ....

(6) .... on a Sunday morning, when the store is usually very quiet. (7) .... are always very friendly and they always try to help you find what you want.

b) Write a similar paragraph about a store you know. Write about

• what the store is called and where it is
• what it sells
• why you like it
• opening times
• the best time to go there
• the people there

Use some of the phrases from the box above.

Listen and read

11 📼 Listen and read about three machines you can buy to make your life easier. Which machine is ...

a the most useful?
   The Bryson D838 Robot
   Vacuum Cleaner

b the cheapest?
   ....
   ....

c the most useful for cooking ideas?
   ....
   ....

d the most expensive?
   ....
   ....

e the smallest?
   ....
   ....

f the best one for people who hate housework?
   ....
   ....

The three most intelligent machines for your home...

Thanks to computer chips, you can now buy machines that can think!!
Here are some of the best machines, which can really make your life easier.

The Bryson D838 Robot Vacuum Cleaner

Do you like housework? No? Then this new robot vacuum cleaner is the machine for you. It can clean your living room automatically. It has a computer that tells it to go around objects such as chairs and table legs as it cleans your floor. And if a person – or your pet dog or cat – comes too close, it stops automatically. The Bryson D838 Robot Vacuum Cleaner comes with electric batteries, and costs £1,800.

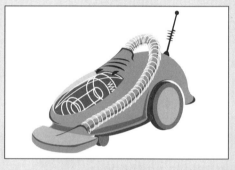

The Freezolux Smart Fridge

A fridge that tells you what it's got inside ... and gives you ideas about what to cook for dinner!! A visual display shows you what's inside the fridge – you don't even have to open the door, and the fridge can also tell you when food is too old to use. And if you don't have any ideas about what to cook for your family this evening ... just touch the computer screen on the door of the fridge, and you can look at over a thousand of your favorite recipes. You can also use it to send emails and to surf the Internet. The Freezolux Smart Fridge is more than just a fridge and costs only £999!

The Ultimate Power Control System

How many remote control units do you have in your house ... for the TV, the video, the CD player ... now you can control everything in your house – from a light in the bedroom to your front door – using just one special remote control unit. It works with radio signals so you can do everything in your house without getting out of bed. You can even surf the Internet, send emails, watch videos, or listen to a CD with the Ultimate Power Control System's video screen. Price – £45. Buy now!!

Vocabulary booster: a supermarket

12 **a)** Label the things in the picture with words from the box.

checkout clerk shopping list customer shopping cart
shopping basket ~~cash register~~ line cans plastic bags

1 ....
2 ....
3 *cash register* ....
4 ....
5 ....
6 ....
7 ....
8 ....
9 ....
10 ....

b) 📼 Listen to the pronunciation of the words on the recording.
Practice saying them.

Spelling

-ing forms

> **LOOK!**
>
> most verbs
> add *-ing*
> *He's flying to Spain.*
>
> verbs ending in *-e*
> take away the *-e*
> *She's making dinner.*
>
> verbs ending consonant +
> vowel + consonant
> double the final consonant
> *She's sitting there.*

1 Write the *-ing* form of these verbs.

a read   *reading*........

b study   ....

c wash   ....

d leave   ....

e come   ....

f stop   ....

g look   ....

h dance   ....

i stay   ....

j give   ....

k plan   ....

l drive   ....

Present Continuous

2 a) Look at the picture. Write what the people are doing, using the verbs.

1 The robot *is cleaning*......... (*clean*) the living room.

2 Veronica .... (*look*) out of the window.

3 She .... (*talk*) to someone on her cellphone.

4 The baby .... (*sit*) on the floor.

5 The baby .... (*eat*) the flowers.

6 Ronald .... (*have*) a cup of tea.

7 He .... (*watch*) television.

8 The two older children .... (*do*) their homework.

b) 🖭 Listen to the sentences on the recording. Practice saying them.

Question words

3 **a)** Write the correct question words in the following sentences and match them to their answers in the box below.

1 ....*What*...... are you doing?
My homework.

2 .... are you going?

....

3 .... are you smiling?

....

4 .... are you talking to?

....

5 .... are you reading?

....

6 .... are you watching?

....

Because you look so funny!   My brother.
Oh, nothing, just a magazine.   To my English class.
Ssh!! It's my favorite program.   ~~My homework~~

b) 📼 Listen to the questions and answers on the recording. Practice saying them.

Short answers

4

> **Short answers with the Present Continuous** ^(LOOK!)
>
> **Are you** going home?   Yes, **I am/we are**.
>   No, **I'm/we're not**.
>
> **Are they** going home?   Yes, **they are**.
>   No, **they aren't**.
>
> **Is he/she** listening?   Yes, **he/she is**.
>   No, **he/she isn't**.
>
> **Notice!** We do not use contracted forms in **positive** short answers.
>
> *Yes, I am.* **not** *~~Yes, I'm.~~*

Write short answers to these questions.

a   Are you enjoying the party, Jo?
     Yes, I am............

b   Is it raining outside?
     No, ...

c   Are your friends staying in this hotel?
     Yes, ...

d   Are you two coming with us?
     Yes, ...

e   Are you waiting to see the doctor, madam?
     No, ...

f   Is Thomas driving?
     Yes, ...

g   Is she talking to us?
     No, ...

All forms

5 **a)** Put the verb in parentheses into the correct form of the Present Continuous: positive, negative, question form, or short answer.

SOPHIE: It's me, Sophie.

JENNY: Hi, Sophie. Where are you? What (1) ...*are you doing*........ (*you/do*)?

SOPHIE: I'm at my sister's wedding.

JENNY: Fantastic! (2) .... (*you/enjoy*) yourself?

SOPHIE: No, (3) ....!! (4) .... (*I/not/have*) a good time. It's awful!!

JENNY: Why? What (5) .... (*happen*)?

SOPHIE: Well, there's the music for a start. (6) .... (*They/play*) this awful 80s music ... and ... oh no, I don't believe it ... my dad (7) .... (*dance*) with my mom's sister.

JENNY: How about your mom? (8) .... (*she/dance*) too?

SOPHIE: No, (9) .... (10) .... (*She/not/do*) anything. (11) .... (*She/look*) at my dad.

JENNY: Oh dear!!

SOPHIE: Just a minute ... there's a very nice young man over there. There's a girl talking to him but (12) he .... (*not/listen*) ... and ... oh!!

JENNY: Sophie. What (13) .... (*he/do*)?

SOPHIE: He (14) .... (*come*) over ... Talk to you later ... Bye!!

b) 📼 Listen to the conversation on the recording.

Present Continuous and Present Simple

6 Underline the best form of the verb, Present Simple or Present Continuous.

a Can I speak to Jane Parsons, please?
– Sorry, she's not in the office today. *She works/She's working* at home today.

b Where *do you come/are you coming* from?
– I'm Italian ... from Milan.

c *Do you speak/Are you speaking* Japanese?
– Just a little.

d Don't forget your umbrella! *It's raining/It rains* again.

e Can you help me with the dinner?
– Not now ... *I watch/I'm watching* TV.

f In Britain, cars *drive/are driving* on the left.

g Hello!! What *do you do/are you doing* here?
– *I'm waiting/I wait* for a friend.

h Can I look at the newspaper now? *Are you reading/Do you read* it?

i Can I phone you back later? *We're having/We have* dinner.

Vocabulary

Describing people

7 Match the words on the right to the definitions on the left.

a A piece of jewelry that you wear in your ear.

b A head where all – or nearly all – the hair is cut.

c The hair on a man's face under his mouth.

d Attractive: nice to look at.

e (for a person) The opposite of small or short.

f Thin, in a good way.

g You wear these if you can't see very well.

h Hair that is yellow or light-colored.

i You use them to see things.

j The hair on a man's face above his mouth.

k Hair that is brown or black.

l Hair that you tie together at the back of your head.

1 tall

2 dark

3 good-looking

4 glasses

5 shaved

6 blonde

7 ~~earring~~

8 ponytail

9 slim

10 beard

11 mustache

12 eyes

a ..7.......... d .... g .... j ....

b .... e .... h .... k ....

c .... f .... i .... l ....

's

8 **a)** Write 's in the correct place in the Column A sentences below.

A	B
1 My sister.'s. in her mid-twenties.	....is........
2 Everybody says she very good-looking.	....
3 Where Frank going?	....
4 Who the girl with long dark hair?	....
5 Dina hair is short.	....
6 David mother doesn't wear glasses.	....
7 Ann the black girl with medium-length hair.	....
8 Maria waiting for me in the car.	....
9 My father mustache looks funny.	....
10 What color are Barbara earrings?	....

b) Is 's: *is* or possessive in each sentence? Complete Column B.

Vocabulary

Clothes

9 Look at the pictures of Bob, Paul, and Marie. Who is wearing ...

a sneakers? ...Bob..........

b a skirt? ....

c a coat? ....

d a tie? ....

e black shoes? ....

f earrings? ....

g a shirt? ....

h jeans? ....

i a suit? ....

j pants? ....

k a white jacket? ....

l a sweater? ....

Bob

Paul

Marie

Listen and read

10 📼 Read and listen to the text about street style, and complete the table.

	Where is she from?	What clothes does she talk about?	Where did she buy her clothes?
Mina	London		
Gloria		dress, pants, shoes	
Alice			Milan, New York

Street Style

This week we went to South Molton Street to find out what young people are wearing when they go shopping.

⬍	**Site Map**
	News
	Chat room
	Horoscopes
	email

Mina is from London: she's a student at the London College of Fashion.

"I'm wearing a pair of jeans from Michiko – it's a Japanese store here in London."

"I love Japanese clothes. The sweater is from Space, and I bought the jacket at Camden Market a couple of weeks ago. My bag and shoes were presents from my family. I like wearing clothes that are different, so I don't usually go shopping in big stores."

Gloria is a designer from Barcelona, in Spain. She's spending a few days here in London. "Because I'm a designer, I love making clothes for myself. I made this dress, and these pants, too. My shoes are from Spain, too ... they're my favorite shoes, but I can't remember where I bought them!"

"I'm looking for a bag that looks good with these clothes. I love shopping in London, but it's very expensive!"

Alice is from the United States. She works for an airline company. "I travel a lot because of my job: I love my work because I can go shopping in lots of wonderful places."

"I bought this top in Milan, and my pants and shoes are from New York. As well as Italy and the United States, I love shopping here in London, too. I'm going to a store called Puzzle – it's near here – to buy myself a new jacket."

Improve your writing

Correcting mistakes

11 Read the description of the picture.
There are twelve mistakes <u>underlined</u>: correct them.

There (a) <u>is</u>/*are* five people in the picture. They are all (b) <u>siting</u> outside: it's a nice day and the sun is (c) <u>shineing</u>. Perhaps they (d) <u>is</u> all on vacation together. One of the men is (e) <u>wearring</u> a suit. One man is behind the others: (f) <u>she's</u> reading a book. The woman in the front (g) <u>have</u> got a newspaper, but she (h) <u>don't</u> reading it. Her (i) <u>eye</u> are closed: perhaps (j) <u>she</u> sleeping. I like this picture: the people (k) <u>looks</u> calm and happy and the scenery is very (l) <u>atractive</u>.

Pronunciation

Stress in questions

12 **a)** 🔲 Listen to the pronunciation of the question words, and the questions with the Present Continuous.

1 What   What are you doing?

2 What   What are they doing?

3 What   What's he doing? What's she doing?

4 Where   Where are you going?

5 Where   Where are they going?

6 Where   Where's he going? Where's she going?

b) 🔲 Listen again and practice saying the questions.

module 11

can/can't for ability

1 **a)** Look at the information about four students: Caroline, Fabrizio, Kristina, and Max.

Caroline

Fabrizio

Kristina

Max

	speak French	play chess	drive a car	play a musical instrument
Caroline	✓	✗	✗	✓
Fabrizio	✓	✓	✗	✗
Kristina	✗	✗	✓	✓
Max	✗	✓	✓	✗

b) Complete the sentences about Caroline and Fabrizio.

1 Caroline ..*can*............... speak French.

2 She ..*can't*............... play chess.

3 .... drive a car.

4 .... play a musical instrument.

5 Fabrizio ....

6 He ....

7 ....

8 ....

c) 📼 Listen to the sentences on the recording. Practice saying them.

Questions and short answers

2

> **LOOK!**
>
> Short answers with *can/can't*
>
> **Can** I/you/he/she/we/they **ask a question?**
>
> **Yes**, I/you/he/she/we/they **can**.
> **No**, I/you/he/she/we/they **can't**.

a) Look back at the information about Kristina and Max. Write the questions and short answers.

1 ..*Can Kristina speak French?*....
...*No, she can't.*...................

2 ....
....

3 ....
....

4 ....
....

5 ....
....

6 ....
....

7 ....
....

8 ....
....

b) 📼 Listen to the questions and answers on the recording. Practice saying them.

Question words

3 Complete the questions below with the correct question word(s) from the box.

> ~~Where~~ What kind How
> What time What color
> What When Which

a *Where*........... is Brisbane?
   It's in Australia.

b .... of tree is that?
   It's a palm tree.

c .... did you go to South America?
   Four years ago.

d .... is your coat?
   The black one.

e *What time*. is your new car?
   White.

f .....*How*....... do we arrive in New York?
   At about three o'clock.

g ....'s your sister's name?
   Maria.

h .... do I turn this off?
   Press the red button.

4 **a)** Read the text below.

Ships of the desert

Perhaps they aren't the most beautiful animals in the world ... but in the hot lands of North Africa and the Middle East they are certainly one of the most useful. How much do you know about camels?

Camels normally live for about 40 years – but they usually stop working when they are about 25.

Camels don't normally like running – it's too hot – but when they need to, they can run at 20 kilometers an hour. The dromedary, or Arabian camel, has one hump. The Bactrian, or Asian camel, has longer hair and has two humps. There are about 14 million camels in the world, and most of them are <u>dromedaries</u>.

An adult camel is about 2.1 meters tall and weighs about 500 kilograms. Camels can walk for more than 600 kilometers without drinking. They only need to drink water every six or eight days. But when there is water, they can drink up to 90 liters.

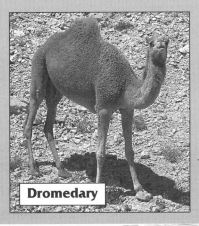

Dromedary

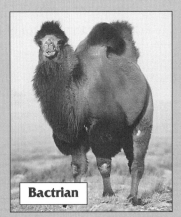

Bactrian

b) Write the questions for this information.

1 *How long do camels live?*

For about 40 years.

2 How ....

About twenty kilometers an hour.

3 How ....

One.

4 How ....

About 14 million.

5 How ....

About 2.1 meters.

6 How ....

About 500 kilograms.

7 How *much* ....

More than 600 kilometers.

8 How ....

Every six or eight days.

9 How ....

Up to 90 liters.

5 Complete the sentences with *how much, how many, which,* or *what.*

a *What* .... do you study at college?

b *How many* .. aunts and uncles have you got?

c There's chocolate or vanilla ice cream for dessert. .... do you prefer?

d .... milk do you want in your coffee?

e There's a bus at nine o'clock and another one at eleven o'clock. .... is better for you?

f .... time did you spend in Africa?

g .... people were there at the meeting?

h .... does a kilo of cheese cost?

i .... is the capital of Romania?

Word order in questions

6 Put the words in the questions into the correct order.

a are there – in – How – many – the US – states ?

How many states are there in the US?

b did – movies – How many – make – he ?

....

c a soccer game – does – How – last – long ?

....

d the boxer – Muhammad Ali – born – was – Where ?

....

e it from – How far – here – to your home – is ?

....

f do – of – What kind – like – you – music ?

....

g can – a – cheetah – fast – run – How ?

....

h the world – is – in – the biggest – ocean – What ?

....

Articles

7 The questions below all come from the general knowledge quiz on pages 94 and 95 of the *Students' Book*. Complete the questions with *a, an,* or *the.*

a Where was *the* Hollywood actor Arnold Schwarzenegger born?

b How many players are there in .... basketball team?

c How long does it take to boil .... egg?

d When did Bill Clinton become president of .... United States?

e What is .... biggest desert in .... world?

f When did Joseph Niépce invent .... first camera?

g How far is it from .... Earth to .... Moon?

h When did France win .... World Cup in soccer?

i *Sushi* is .... popular type of food. Where does it come from?

Vocabulary booster: animals

8 **a)** How many of the animals below can you name?
Write the word next to the correct number below.

duck   frog   mouse   dog   cow   sheep   monkey   horse   honeybees   beetle   snake   spider

1	5	9 ....
2	6	10 ....
3	7	11 ....
4	8	12 ....

b) 📼 Listen to the pronunciation of the words on the recording. Practice saying them.

c) Put the animals into one of the groups below.

Animals with no legs   *snake*......

Animals with two legs   ....

Animals with four legs   ....

                              ....

Animals with more than four legs   ....

Listen and read

9 📼 Read and listen to the text about the animal world, and find out the following questions.

a About how many animals species are there in the world? *ten million* ....

b How tall can an adult giraffe grow? ....

c How long is the smallest mammal, Savi's pygmy shrew? ....

d How much does a goliath frog weigh? ....

e How tall is an adult ostrich? ....

f How fast can a bee hummingbird move its wings? ....

g How many types of kangaroo are there? ....

h How many bison were/are there in America in:
   i) the mid 1860s ....
   ii) the mid 1880s ....
   iii) now? ....

The Animal World

We do not know how many species of animals there are, as people are discovering new ones all the time; but most scientists think that there are about ten million different animal species in the world.

Giraffes are the tallest animals on Earth. A large adult male giraffe can be up to 6 meters tall. Thanks to its long legs and neck, it can eat the leaves from the tops of trees.

The smallest animals are called protozoa, which have only one cell, and are so small that we cannot see them without a powerful microscope.

The smallest mammal is Savi's pygmy shrew – it is only 6 centimeters long, including its tail.

The goliath frog (*Rana Goliath*) of West Africa can be up to 75 centimeters long, and weighs about 3 kilograms. The goliath beetle is probably the world's largest beetle – it weighs more than 100 grams – about the same as two eggs.

■ Protozoa

■ Shrew

■ Bison

■ Ostrich

■ Hummingbird

The ostrich is the world's largest bird. An adult ostrich is more than 2.5 meters tall, but it cannot fly.

The bee hummingbird is probably the world's smallest bird – it is just 5 centimeters long and weighs less than 2 grams; it can stay still in the air by moving its wings twenty to fifty times per second. One of the largest birds that can fly is the South American condor; its wings are 3 meters from end to end.

There are more than fifty different types of kangaroo in Australia. When it is born, a baby kangaroo is less than 2.5 centimeters long, but an adult kangaroo can grow to more than 2 meters in height.

In the mid 1860s, there were about 13 million bison living in North America. By the mid 1880s, there were only a few hundred. Today there are about 50,000 bison in America, living in special parks.

More about numbers

10 a) Put the words into numbers.

1 sixty thousand   *60,000*
2 nineteen eighty-five   ....
3 three thousand   ....
4 ninety kilometers an hour   ....
5 nine point six   ....
6 two hundred and fifty-three thousand   ....
7 sixty-two million   ....
8 two hundred and ninety-seven   ....
9 two billion   ....
10 nine hundred and sixty-three   ....

b) Put the numbers into words.

1 53,000   *fifty-three thousand*
2 150km/h
3 3,000,000
4 8.5
5 348
6 2,000,000,000
7 5,600
8 1980
9 350,000
10 80,000,000

Pronunciation

Numbers

11 a) 🔲 Listen to the pronunciation of these words. Practice saying them.

| nine | nineteen | hundred | thousand |
| million | billion | | |

b) 🔲 Listen to the pronunciation of the numbers in Exercise 10a. Practice saying them.

c) 🔲 Practice saying the words in Exercise 10b. Listen to the recording to check.

Improve your writing

Apostrophes, periods, and question marks

12

> **LOOK!**
>
> **We use apostrophes:**
> • in contracted forms:
>   *she's can't doesn't*
> • with possessive 's:
>   *John's friend the world's favorite airline*
>
> **We use periods at the end of statements.**
> *They're French. I'm fine.*
>
> **We use question marks at the end of questions.**
> *Where do you live? Where is it?*

Write apostrophes, periods, and question marks in the sentences below.

a Dogs can only see black and white – they can't see colors.
b Im not sure what the answer is
c Is it true that koala bears dont drink water
d What is the worlds largest animal
e He doesnt know the answer
f Wheres the biggest lake in the world
g What is Peters pet dogs name

module 12

Future plans

going to

1 a) Look at the pictures and write a sentence about what the people are going to do. Use the phrases in the box.

have lunch	~~have a baby~~	stop	get wet

buy a newspaper   paint the ceiling   go to bed
play tennis

1 *She's going to have a baby.*.................

2 He ....

3 They ....

4 The bus ....

5 They ....

6 He ....

7 They ....

8 They ....

b) 🔲 Listen to the answers on the recording. Practice saying them.

want to

2 Complete the sentences with the correct form of *want to*: positive, question, or negative. Use the words in brackets.

a *Do you want to* .... (*you*) rent a video this evening? There's nothing good on TV.

b No, I'm really not hungry.
.... (*I*) eat anything, thank you.

c Valerie is going to look for a job when she leaves school. .... (*she*) go to college.

d .... (*anybody*) go for a cup of coffee when the lesson finishes?

e .... (*your friends*) go for a walk before we have dinner?

f Patricia is very, very tired.
.... (*she*) go home and go to bed.

g .... (*he*) be a waiter, but it was the only job he could find.

h .... (*you*) anything to eat with your coffee?

would like to and want to

3 a) Rearrange the words to make sentences with *want to* or *would like to*.

1 would like – a soccer player – to be – when he's older – Stephen
Stephen would like to be a soccer player when he's older.

2 you – something – like – to drink? – Would
....

3 and I – a table – near – My friends – the window, please – would like
....

4 want – doesn't – stay – at home – to – Marc
....

5 this evening? – to see – like – movie – Which – would you
....

6 a – taxi – order – I'd – to – please – like
....

7 coffee, – We – thank you – any more – want – don't
....

8 in the park? – you – Would – like – to go – for a walk
....

b) 🔈 Listen to the sentences on the recording. Practice saying them.

Future forms

4 Write **one** extra word in the sentences below. would

a Françoise/like to go to Japan one day.

b Tomorrow's Saturday ... I going to stay in bed all day.

c Where do you want go?

d Would you to go out for lunch?

e Chris isn't enjoying his vacation: he to go home!!

f My friends are going cook a special meal this evening.

g What would you like do tomorrow?

h We not going to have a vacation this year.

Vocabulary

Ways to spend the weekend

5 Complete the words to make words or phrases to express the opposite.

a It was boring! It was g _o_ o d f _u_ n!

b a busy weekend a q _ _ _ t weekend.

c a relaxing day a t _ _ _ _ g day

d stay in go _ _ _

e get up s _ _ y in b _ _

f never a _ _ _ _ s

Word combinations with *go*, *have*, *stay*

6 Find the correct words or phrases in the box.

a concert	a novel	the gym
children	television	at home
in bed	sports	an exhibition
a museum	the movies

~~children~~

a who can you **look after**?

children

b what five things can you **go to**?

....

....

....

....

....

c where can you **stay** (two places)?

....

....

d what can you **watch** (two things)?

....

....

e what can you can **read**?

....

Suggestions and offers

7 a) Mark, Barbara, and their two children are on a camping holiday in the mountains. Complete the conversation with one of the words or phrases from the box.

| ~~shall~~ | see | Let's | I'll | about | idea | could | like | we | don't want |

MARK: Well, everybody ... what (1) .*shall*.......... we do today? Any ideas?

SUSIE: I'm not sure ... it depends on the weather. Is it sunny outside?

MARK: Just a minute ... no, not exactly ... in fact, it's raining again.

JAKE: Oh no! I (2) .... another boring day like yesterday. Is there something interesting we can go and see?

BARBARA: I know what we can do. (3) .... have a look at the guidebook. I'm sure we can find some ideas in there.

MARK: All right. Where is the guidebook?

SUSIE: It's there, next to your feet.

MARK: Let's (4) .... well, there's the Museum of Country Life; how (5) .... that?

JAKE: Hmm ... is there anything more exciting?

MARK: Well, we (6) .... go to Aqua World. It's a sea life center.

JAKE: Yes, that sounds better. Shall (7) .... go there?

SUSIE: OK, then, if you (8) ....

BARBARA: Shall I phone them to see what time it opens?

MARK: Good (9) ....! So, everybody's happy. (10) .... make some more coffee and then we can all get ready.

b) 🖭 Listen to the conversation and check your answers.

Pronunciation

I'll, we'll

8 a) 🔲 Listen to the pairs of sentences below. Notice the pronunciation of *'ll*.

1 I open the window.   I'll open the window.
2 I turn on the heating.   I'll turn on the heating.
3 We make lunch for you.   We'll make lunch for you.
4 I phone for a taxi.   I'll phone for a taxi.
5 I drive.   I'll drive.
6 We buy some bread.   We'll buy some bread.

b) 🔲 Practice saying the sentences. Copy the voices.

Future time expressions

9 a) It is 9 a.m. on Wednesday. Write the future time expressions in order.

| tonight ~~this afternoon~~ tomorrow evening next month next year |
| tomorrow morning next week this weekend |

9 a.m. Wednesday
this afternoon.........
....
....
....
....
....
....
....

b) It is now 4 p.m. on Friday, April 10, 2001. What's another way to say ...

1 10 a.m., Saturday, April 11?   ....
2 9 p.m., Saturday?   ....
3 The week April 13–17?   ....
4 Saturday and Sunday, April 11 and 12? ....
5 May 2001?   ....
6 2002?   ....
7 10 p.m., Friday, April 10?   ....

Talking about the weather

10 Read the sentences and describe the weather.

a You're going to need your umbrellas if you go out.
   It's raining./It's wet..................

b Can you pass me my sunglasses ... that's better. Now I can see!!
   ....

c Thirty-five degrees!! Let's go for a swim!
   ....

d Please drive carefully – in some places you can't see more than five meters.
   ....

e What a beautiful spring day. Let's go for a walk!
   ....

f The weather's not too bad today. There's no sun, but it isn't raining.
   ....

g Look outside! The garden is completely white!!
   ....

h Put on your warm clothes if you go out!
   ....

i All the leaves are falling off the trees!!
   ....

Prepositions

11 Complete the sentences with *in*, *on*, *to*, or *at*.

a   Paul never goes out .*on*..... weekends.

b   Let's go .... the movies!

c   There's a party .... my house on Saturday. Can you come?

d   I'm so tired. I'm going to stay .... bed all day tomorrow.

e   The weather can get really hot .... summer.

f   I didn't go out at all this weekend: I just stayed .... home as usual.

g   Martina and I went .... a rock concert on Saturday – it was great!

h   We went to the United States .... vacation a few years ago.

Listen and read

12   Read and listen to the world weather report for the week ending March 15. Complete the information in the table.

	What was the weather like?	Extra information
Chicago	*snow, windy*	
San Francisco		
Queensland		*475 mm of rain in five days*
Jerez de la Frontera		
The Balkans		
Northeast Italy		
Irkutsk		

The World Weather Report

March 15

There was heavy snow and windy weather in Chicago on Monday, and there was also heavy rain on the west coast of the United States – particularly in and around the city of San Francisco.

Things were no better on the other side of the world in Australia – there was extremely heavy rain in the state of Queensland, with 475 mm of rain falling in just five days.

In southwest Europe, there was more hot, sunny weather with the town of Jerez de la Frontera in the south of Spain the hottest place. The temperature was 30 degrees, the warmest so far this year.

It wasn't all good news in Europe, however. There was heavy snow in the Balkans, and parts of northeast Italy on Monday and Tuesday. Things are getting a little better in the city of Irkutsk, in eastern Siberia, however: the temperature went above zero degrees for the first time since last November.

Vocabulary

Definitions

13 Use the definition to write in the word. You can find all the words in Module 12 of the *Students' Book*.

a A book that tells a story about imaginary people.

N O V E L

b A place where people grow grapes.

V _ _ _ _ _ _ _

c A place where you go for physical exercise.

G _ _

d A time when people meet and enjoy themselves.

P _ _ _ _

e A way of agreeing to a suggestion.

GOOD   I _ _ _ !

f A way of making a suggestion.

L _ _ ' _   GO!

g A word for people in your family.

R _ _ _ _ _ _ _ _

h A word for Saturday and Sunday.

W _ _ _ _ _ _

i Breakfast, lunch, and dinner are all ...

M _ _ _ _

j Extra work that you do after school.

H _ _ _ _ _ _ _

k It means "not interesting."

B _ _ _ _ _

l To take care of.

LOOK   A _ _ _ _

m This is between the afternoon and the night.

E _ _ _ _ _ _

n This is what you do when you move through water using your arms and legs.

S _ _ _

o This is when you go to hear people playing music.

C _ _ _ _ _ _

p This is when you move your body to music.

D _ _ _ _

q You see these at the movie theater.

M _ _ _ _ _

r You are this when you want to drink something.

T _ _ _ _ _ _

Improve your writing

Writing about a popular vacation resort

14 **a)** Make notes about a popular vacation resort in your country under these headings:

Where it is
The most important attractions
Places to eat and drink
Things to do for children
Excursions

b) Write a paragraph about the resort using some of the phrases in the box.

> ... is in the north/south/east/west of ...
> It's one of the (oldest/most interesting/most beautiful) towns in ...
> It has a large number of ...
> The best ... is ... which has ...
> There are lots of places to ...
> You can enjoy ...
> For children there is ...
> You can also visit ...

module 13

Present Perfect

1 Complete the sentences with the Present Perfect form of the verbs in parentheses.

a Karen's parents
have lived......... in Scotland
all their lives. (*live*)

b J. R. Cowling ....
more than twenty books.
(*write*)

c Sixty percent of people in
the United States
.... never
.... abroad. (*go*)

d Martin ....
hundreds of emails to Kyla –
she's his favorite singer.
(*send*)

e My friend and I
.... all of Steven
Spielberg's movies. (*see*)

f I .... never
.... a Ferrari ...
but I'd like to!! (*drive*)

g Because of her job, Diana
.... a lot of
famous people. (*meet*)

h Do you like Japanese food?
– I don't know. I
.... never
.... it. (*try*)

Positive and negative

2 **a)** The first Women's Soccer World Cup was in China in 1991. There have been three more World Cups: here are the winners and the losing finalists.

Year	Venue	Winners	Goals	Losing finalists	Goals
1991	China	United States	2	Norway	1
1995	Sweden	Norway	2	Germany	0
1999	US	United States (*United States won on penalties*)	0	China	0
2003	US	Germany	2	Sweden	1

b) Complete the sentences with the Present Perfect of the verb.

1 There _have been_......... (*be*) four World Cups up to now.

2 The United States .... (*win*) the competition twice.

3 They .... (*not/have*) the competition in South America.

4 Germany .... (*play*) in two World Cup finals.

5 The United States .... (*never/lose*) in the final.

6 There .... (*be*) one World Cup in Europe.

7 Norway and the United States .... (*play*) in two finals.

8 Germany .... (*win*) the World Cup once.

9 Norway .... (*score*) three goals in the World Cup finals.

10 There .... (*be*) one final that finished in a penalty shoot-out.

Questions and short answers

LOOK!

Short answers with the Present Perfect
Have you/I/we/they **done it**?
Yes, I/you/we/they **have**.
No, I/you/we/they **haven't**.

Has he/she/it **done it**?
Yes, he/she/it **has**.
No, he/she/it **hasn't**.

3 **a)** Read about the people below. Then complete the questions and write the correct short answer.

Richard Marshall and his wife Elaine are retired. Recently they moved to a new house in Hexham, a town near Newcastle, in the north of England. Richard was born in Hexham, but Elaine is originally from Aberdeen, a town in the north of Scotland.

Gordon Marshall – Richard and Elaine's son – was born in Newcastle but he now lives with his wife and daughter in Leeds, a town about 150 km away, where he is a teacher. He's also worked abroad – he worked in a restaurant in France when he was younger.

Sarah Marshall – Gordon's wife – has always wanted her own business. Her daughter Rebecca left school last year, and now they're in business together. She and her mother have opened a new sandwich store called Crusts in downtown Leeds. It's the first time they've worked together!

1   _Has_.... Richard always lived in Hexham?
    Yes, he has............

2   .... Elaine ever lived in another town?
    ....

3   .... they always lived in the same house?
    ....

4   .... Gordon always been a teacher?
    ....

5   .... he ever worked abroad?
    ....

6   .... Gordon and Sarah always lived in Leeds?
    ....

7   .... Sarah had her own business before?
    ....

8   .... Rebecca left school?
    ....

b) 📠 Listen to the sentences on the recording. Practice saying them.

Irregular past participles

4 **a)** Find the past participles of the verbs. What is the mystery word?

sleep	_S_	_L_	_E_	_P_	_T_			
make			–	–	–	–		
lose		–	–	–	–			
stand			–	–	–	–	–	
speak			–	–	–	–		–
take			–	–	–	–	–	
drive			–	–	–	–	–	–
write	–	–	–	–	–	–	–	
say		–	–	–	–			
come			–	–	–	–		
give			–	–	–	–		
keep		–	–	–	–			
tell		–	–	–	–			
become			–	–	–	–	–	
see				–	–	–	–	

b) 📠 Listen to the pronunciation of the verbs on the recording. Practice saying them.

Spelling
Regular past participles

5

> To form the past participle of regular verbs we add -ed:
> play ➡ played
>
> If the regular verb ends in -e we add -d only:
> decide ➡ decided
>
> The verbs say and pay take -aid:
> say ➡ said
> pay ➡ paid
>
> Verbs ending in the consonant + -y change the -y to -ied:
> study ➡ studied
> try ➡ tried

LOOK!

Look at the sentences below. Is the spelling of the past participle correct or not? If it is incorrect, write the correct spelling.

a Have you ever **staid** in an expensive hotel? .X.
  .stayed.....

b Have you **used** this kind of computer before? .....
  ....

c I've never **tryed** Japanese tea before. It's delicious!!   .....
  ....

d We haven't **decided** where to go on vacation......
  ....

e My mother has always **studyed** music.   .....
  ....

f Exams have never **worried** me.   .....
  ....

g Have you ever **plaid** baseball?   .....
  ....

h I've **livd** in this apartment all my life.   .....
  ....

ever, before, never, always

6 Complete the gaps with always, before, ever, or never.

a I don't know what this is: I haven't eaten it
  before...........

b Laura has .... wanted to be a doctor: it's her ambition.

c Have you .... met anyone famous?

d Is this your first visit to Oxford.
  – No, it isn't. I've been here ....

e I've .... liked pop music: I prefer jazz.

f Have you tried Indian food .... , or is this the first time?

g We're very happy with our car; we've .... had any problems with it.

h Have you .... slept outside all night?

Definite and zero article

7 Complete the sentences with the or Ø.

a We often have dinner in *Luigi's*: _the_..... pizzas are really good there.

b What was .... name of .... man who invented television?

c Did you see .... soccer game on TV last night?

d Which are usually cheaper? .... apples or .... oranges?

e Can I have a cup of tea, please? I don't drink .... coffee.

f I'm sorry, I can't hear you – .... music is too loud!!

g Do you take .... sugar in your coffee?

h We had a good vacation, but .... weather wasn't very good.

Articles: *a*, *an*, and *the*

8 a) Complete the joke with *a*, *an*, or *the*.

Once upon (1) *a*........ time there was (2) .... lion. He felt very happy with himself that day, so he decided to go for (3) .... walk in (4) .... jungle. After (5) .... few minutes, he met (6) .... snake.

"Who is (7) .... king of (8) .... jungle?" asked (9) .... lion.

"You are, of course," replied (10) .... snake. (11) .... lion felt even happier.

Next, (12) .... lion came to (13) .... big river. Sitting in (14) .... river, there was (15) .... crocodile.

"Who is (16) .... king of the jungle?" (17) .... lion asked (18) .... crocodile.

"You are, of course," answered (19) .... crocodile, and swam away.

(20) .... lion continued his walk. All (21) .... animals he met agreed that (22) .... lion was (23) .... king of (24) .... jungle.

Finally, he met (25) .... elephant.

"Who is (26) .... king of (27) .... jungle?" asked (28) .... lion.

(29) .... elephant didn't say anything, but he picked up (30) .... lion in his enormous trunk, and threw him into (31) .... air.

"All right, all right," said (32) .... lion, "Don't get angry just because you don't know (33) .... answer."

b) 🖅 Listen to the joke and check your answers.

Vocabulary

Ways of communicating

9 What are these instructions for? Choose one of the phrases from the box.

> ~~leaving a phone message~~   sending an email
> making a telephone call   buying online
> surfing the Internet   sending a card
> writing a letter   sending a fax

a "After you hear a BEEP, speak slowly and clearly. Don't forget to say your name ..."
   leaving a phone message
   ....

b Write your address and the date in the top right corner. Start with *Dear* and the name of the ...
   ....

c When you've finished your writing, click on the *Send* button at the top of the screen.
   ....

d Put the document into the machine ... then dial the number and press the button which ...
   ....

e Click on the item you want ... then you have to give your address and credit card details ...
   ....

f ... if you can't find the information you want, click on *Links* and you'll see a list of other websites.
   ....

g Press the green button, and you'll hear a tone ... then dial the phone number. Don't forget the code.
   ....

h Don't forget to write your name inside! Then put it in an envelope, write the address, and mail it.
   ....

Vocabulary booster: the mail

10 **a)** Match a word from the box to the correct picture.

postcard   birthday card   mailbox   parcel
envelope   invitation   stamps   note   mailman
mailing a letter

1 *postcard* ....   5 ....   9 ....
2 ....   6 ....   10 ....
3 ....   7 ....
4 ....   8 ....

b) 🔲 Listen to the pronunciation of the words on the recording. Practice saying them.

Pronunciation

Past participles

11 **a)** Look at the list of past participles below. <u>Underline</u> the sound that has a different pronunciation.

1	sent	met	m**a**de	said	read
2	done	gone	run	won	beg**u**n
3	made	played	stayed	paid	fed
4	stolen	spoken	told	got	chosen
5	caught	bought	drawn	shown	taught

b) 🔲 Listen to the pronunciation of the words on the recording. Practice saying them.

Improve your writing

Writing a note

12 a) Read the note on the right and answer these questions.

1 Who is it for? _Joe_.....................

2 Who wrote it? ....

3 Where did she go? ....

4 When will she be back? ....

> Hi Joe,
> Hope you had a good day at work!
> Gone to supermarket to get something for dinner. Back at 6.
> See you then.
> Love,
>   Fiona

LOOK!

When we write a note, we often miss out words like:

articles	~~the~~ supermarket
pronouns and auxiliary verbs	~~I~~ hope ... ~~I've~~ gone
and we use shorter forms	6 = 6 o'clock Hi! Thanks = Thank you

b) Tom is on vacation. Charlotte is looking after his cats. Cross out or change the <u>underlined</u> words to make Tom's note for Charlotte.

> Hi
> ~~Good morning~~ Charlotte!
> <u>Thank you very much</u> for feeding <u>the</u> cats!!
> <u>There are some</u> cans of cat food in <u>the</u> cupboard next to <u>the</u> window.
> Please give <u>them</u> one can ONLY!! <u>I'll</u> see you on Saturday, about 1 <u>o'clock</u>.
> Love,
>   Tom

have to, don't have to

1 Bruce, George, Alizia, and Meera all work for GONE!! airline. Complete the sentences about them with *has/have to* or *doesn't/don't have to*.

Bruce is a member of the cabin crew.

a He *has to* .... look after passengers.

b He .... use a computer.

c He .... look well-dressed.

George is a pilot.

d He .... fly the plane.

e He .... serve food.

f He .... wear a uniform.

Alizia and Meera work at the GONE!! call center near London.

g They .... wear a uniform.

h They .... travel a lot.

Questions and short answers

2 a) Write questions as in the example, and give the correct short answer.

> LOOK!
>
> **Short answers with** *have to*
>
> **Do** I/you/we/they **have to** go?
> **Yes**, I/you/we/they **do**.
> **No**, I/you/we/they **don't**.
>
> **Does** he/she/it **have to** go?
> **Yes**, he/she/it **does**.
> **No**, he/she/it **doesn't**.

1 Bruce/have to/look after the passengers?
Does Bruce have to look after the passengers?
Yes, he does.

2 he/have to/use a computer?
....
....

3 he/have to/look well-dressed?
....
....

4 George/have to/fly the plane?
....
....

5 he/have to/serve food?
....
....

6 he/have to/wear a uniform?
....
....

7 Alizia and Meera/have to/wear uniforms?
....
....

8 they/have to/travel a lot?
....
....

b) 🖳 Listen to the sentences on the recording. Practice saying them.

have to, don't have to, can, can't

3 **a)** Look at the information about flights to New York on two airlines – BAC and GONE!! – and complete the sentences with *have to, don't have to, can*, or *can't*.

	BAC	GONE!!
Ticket price	1st class round-trip ticket: £1,500	Standby ticket: £150
Check-in time	1 hour before	be at the airport 3 hours before
Before the flight	special VIP lounge	wait in departure lounge only
Food and drink	yes – free	buy sandwiches and drinks on plane
Inflight film	yes	no
Seats	seat numbers	no seat numbers
duty-free goods	yes	no

On BAC:
1 You *have to* check in one hour before.
2 You .... wait in the VIP lounge.
3 You .... pay for your food and drinks.
4 You .... watch an inflight film.
5 You .... sit in a particular seat.
6 You .... buy duty-free goods.

On GONE!!:
7 You .... arrive at the airport three hours before.
8 You .... wait in the VIP lounge.
9 You .... pay for your food and drinks.
10 You .... watch an inflight film.
11 You .... sit where you want.
12 You .... buy duty-free goods.

b) 📟 Listen to the sentences on the recording. Practice saying them.

Vocabulary

Town facilities

4 Here is a list of places that János wants to visit while he is in Branton. Use the words in the box to answer the questions.

> the park   the art gallery
> the beach   ~~the square~~
> the sports stadium
> the river   the museum
> the shopping center

Where can he:
a sit with a cup of coffee and watch people walk past?
  the square ....
b see paintings?
  ....
c watch an athletics meeting?
  ....
d go shopping?
  ....
e see interesting old objects and learn about history?
  ....
f sunbathe and go swimming?
  ....
g sit and relax in a place with grass and trees?
  ....
h go on a boat trip?
  ....

5

Which A is a place where airplanes take off and land?

Which B goes across a street, railroad line, or a river?

Which C is a large strong building?

Which D is something you ask for when you're lost?

Which E is the opposite of *beginning*

Which F means *wonderful* or *great*?

Which G is a place where you see paintings?

Which H is a small mountain?

Which I is the opposite of *boring*?

Which J is a trip from one place to another?

Which K is 1,000 meters?

Which M is a very high place – the Matterhorn, for example?

When something is N, it means that you have to do it.

Which O is the opposite of *closed*?

Which P is a place in a town with trees, grass, flowers, etc.?

Which R is the Thames, the Amazon, and the Nile?

Which S is a stone model of a famous person?

Which T is something you have to buy when you travel by bus, train, etc.?

Which U is the opposite of *over*?

Which W is a way to get from one place to another using your legs?

A _IRPORT_

B _ _ _ _ _ _

C _ _ _ _ _ _

D _ _ _ _ _ _ _ _ _

E _ _

F _ _ _ _ _ _ _ _

G _ _ _ _ _ _

H _ _ _

I _ _ _ _ _ _ _ _ _ _

J _ _ _ _ _ _

K _ _ _ _ _ _ _ _

M _ _ _ _ _ _ _ _

N _ _ _ _ _ _ _ _ _

O _ _ _

P _ _ _

R _ _ _ _ _

S _ _ _ _ _ _

T _ _ _ _ _ _

U _ _ _ _

W _ _ _

Prepositions of movement

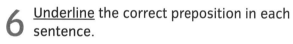

6 <u>Underline</u> the correct preposition in each sentence.

a Walk <u>*along*</u>/*into*/*out of* the main street until you come to the main square.

b If you want to get to the main shopping area, go *into*/*over*/*through* the river to the north of the city.

c It's a long walk *from*/*out of*/*up* the hill, but at the end of it you can see the whole city ... it's wonderful!

d There's a bus stop near the school where you can get a bus *down*/*over*/*into* downtown Dallas.

e The Number Six streetcar goes *across*/*past*/ *through* the door of our apartment.

f You can now fly *across*/*along*/*past* the Atlantic Ocean in less than six hours.

g How long does it take to drive *down*/*from*/*to* here to the coast?

h Most visitors park their cars outside and then walk *along*/*into*/*over* Boston's downtown.

Listen and read

Unusual places to visit

7 🎧 Read and listen to the text about three unusual places to visit, and complete the table below.

	Blue Lagoon	London Bridge	Guggenheim Museums
What it is/they are	....	....	....
Where it is/they are	*45 km from Reykjavik* *Iceland*	....	....
Why people go there	....	....	....

Blue Lagoon – Iceland

Iceland – a country in the North Atlantic near the Arctic Circle – probably isn't the first place you think of for a perfect beach vacation. But every year, thousands of people take off their clothes and swim at the Blue Lagoon, a beach near the Arctic Circle and just 45 km from the capital city, Reykjavik. The air temperature can be as low as –10 degrees: but the water comes from underground and is naturally hot – the usual water temperature is between 35 and 40 degrees. It's like taking a hot bath in the open air!!

London Bridge – USA!!

The original London Bridge actually isn't in London at all ... and it doesn't even pass over a river!! American businessman Robert P. McCulloch bought the bridge for $2.5 million in 1968 and moved it – stone by stone – across the Atlantic Ocean. He rebuilt it in Lake Havasu City, Arizona – a small town in the middle of the desert, where the temperature is often more than 40 degrees. Nowadays, thousands of tourists come to see the bridge, and there is an English village with watersports facilities, stores, and restaurants.

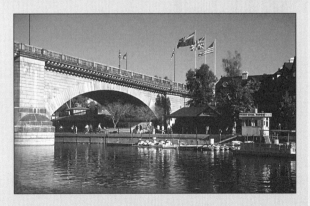

The Guggenheim Museums

There are not one but five Guggenheim Museums. Solomon R. Guggenheim opened the first collection of modern art in New York in 1959. Another museum opened in Venice, and then, in 1997, two more Guggenheims opened: one in Berlin and the other in the Basque city of Bilbao, in the north-west of Spain. It is now one of Spain's biggest tourist attractions, and every year hundreds of thousands of people come to see the paintings and other works of art. The newest Guggenheim museum is the Guggenheim Hermitage Museum in Las Vegas.

Vocabulary booster: a shopping center

an escalator   a stroller   steps   shoppers
a clothes store   a department store   a shop window
automatic doors   ~~an elevator~~   a bench

8 **a)** Label the objects in the picture with words from the box.

an elevator

2 .... 5 .... 8 ....

3 .... 6 .... 9 ....

4 .... 7 .... 10 ....

b) 🖵 Listen to the pronunciation of the words on the recording. Practice saying them.

Spelling and pronunciation

Silent letters

9 **a)** All the words in the box have at least one silent letter. Which letter(s) don't we pronounce? Cross out the silent letters, as in the example.

1	castle	3	scenery	5	building	7	design	9	sights	11	sign
2	straight	4	highest	6	through	8	know	10	right	12	listen

b) 🖵 Listen to the pronunciation of the words on the recording. Practice saying them.

Improve your writing

A postcard

10 **a)** James and Thelma are spending a few days in London. They have written a postcard to their neighbors in the United States. Read the postcard and write the words from the box into the correct space.

~~Hi~~	nearest	have	great
English	seen	Bye	tea	in

(1) ...*Hi*.... everybody!!

Here we are (2) .... London!

The weather isn't too bad and we're having a (3) .... time. We've

(4) .... the Changing of the Guard at Buckingham Palace, and right now we're having a cup of (5) ....

The kids want to go to the (6) .... McDonald's, but Thelma and I want to

(7) .... lunch in a real old

(8) .... pub near Westminster Abbey.

(9) .... for now!

Bob, Thelma, and the kids

The Watts Family
5831 Hills Avenue
Daytoun
Virginia VA 838
USA

b) Choose a place and write a postcard to someone you know. Use some of the phrases below.

Useful language

Here we are in ...   We've seen ...   The weather is(n't) ...

Right now, we're ...   We want to ...   We're having a ...time

We're going to ...   ... want(s) to go to ...   Bye for now!

module 15

Infinitive of purpose

1 Last Friday, Carol went into town. Why did she visit these places? Write sentences with the infinitive of purpose, using the phrases in the box.

> borrow some books   have lunch   buy some meat
> ~~get some money~~   buy some fruit juice
> catch the bus home   visit her sick friend
> send a parcel to her cousin

a   the bank

She went to the bank to get some money.

b   the library

....

c   the post office

....

d   the hospital

....

e   the grocery store

....

f   the butcher's

....

g   the Oak Tree coffee shop.................................

....

h   the bus station

....

might, might not

2 a) Rewrite the sentences using *might* or *might not* instead of the words in **bold**.

1   **Perhaps** we**'ll** go swimming this afternoon.
    We *might go swimming this afternoon.*

2   **It's possible that** the plane **will** arrive late.
    The plane ....

3   **Maybe** you**'ll** be rich one day, if you work hard.
    You ....

4   **It's possible that** I **won't** be able to come to class next week.
    I ....

5   I **possibly won't** see Frank this weekend.
    I ....

6   **Perhaps** Philip **won't** stay until the end of the course.
    Philip ....

7   The government **will possibly** change the education system soon.
    The government ....

8   **Maybe** the exam **won't** be as difficult as you think.
    The exam ....

b) 🖴 Listen to the sentences on the recording. Practice saying them.

will and *won't* (*probably*)

3 a) Rearrange the words to make sentences.

1 probably – another – be – It – tomorrow – will – nice day

   It will probably be another nice day tomorrow.

2 time – won't – There – to stop for lunch – be – probably

   ....

   ....

3 be – will – class – probably – for – late – Martha

   ....

   ....

4 need – your – You – probably – umbrella – won't

   ....

   ....

5 be able – tomorrow – I – to come – won't – probably

   ....

   ....

6 soon – There – probably – be – an election – will

   ....

   ....

b) 📇 Listen to the sentences on the recording. Practice saying them.

might (not), *will*, and *won't*

4 a) Tom, Meg, and Sampath are three school friends who have just finished their exams. Read the notes about their plans for the future.

Tom

Meg

Sampath

	Vacation?	**College?**	**Job?**
Tom	no plans – Greece maybe	maybe not!	my father's company, probably
Meg	probably Spain with my parents	next year, probably	all my family are doctors, so why not me?
Sampath	don't think I'll have time	not sure – perhaps get a job abroad instead	who knows – an actor?

b) Use the information to write sentences with *might*, *might not*, *will probably*, or *probably won't*.

1 Tom *might go to Greece for his vacation.*.......................... (*go to Greece*)

2 Meg .... (*go to Spain*)

3 Sampath .... (*have time for a vacation*)

4 Tom .... (*go to college*)

5 Meg .... (*go to college next year*)

6 Sampath .... (*get a job abroad instead*)

7 Tom .... (*work for his father's company*)

8 Meg .... (*become a doctor*)

9 Sampath .... (*become an actor*)

Infinitives with and without *to*

5 <u>Underline</u> the correct form in the sentences below.

a Taka wants *learn*/<u>*to learn*</u> more about computers.

b Paul is studying English *get*/*to get* a better job.

c It might *be*/*to be* better if you do it yourself.

d I'm going to the supermarket *buy*/*to buy* some bread. Do you want anything?

e Charles probably won't *pass*/*to pass* the exam.

f Thousands of people went to Australia *to watch*/*watch* the Olympics.

g We might not *have*/*to have* a vacation this year.

Vocabulary

Education and learning

6 Complete the text with words from the box.

subjects	take	high	failed	~~elementary~~	doing
qualifications	pass	graduates	at	foreign	

Is there really a big difference between boys and girls at school? New research says there is.

British girls between the ages of five and eleven have always done better at (a) *elementary* school than boys: but now older girls are doing better at (b) .... school too.

Many people think that boys are better (c) .... science and math and that girls do well in (d) .... languages and art. But more and more women are going to college, and (e) .... courses in (f) .... like law and engineering.

Every year, tens of thousands of British teenagers (g) .... their A or (advanced) level exams. These are the exams that young people need to (h) .... if they want to go to college. But in 2000, more boys than girls (i) .... their A levels. Too many young boys leave school with no (j) .... at all. For young men like this, it is very difficult to find a good job these days, when big companies are looking for the best (k) ....

7 Look at the extracts from some children's textbooks. What subject are they about?

~~English~~	Mathematics	Science	Geography
Information Technology	History	Art	Music

Ⓐ *English*

All these words start with *com* (Latin: *with*). See if you know the English meaning. Then check in your dictionary.
complete, compare,

Ⓑ _____

São Paulo, Brazil, is South America's largest city and one of the fastest-growing cities in the world. It is the commercial center of

Ⓒ _____

The memory of a computer consists of microchips. There are two types: ROM (read-only memory) contains permanent instructions,

Ⓓ _____

In the fourteenth century, Arab traders sailed across the Indian Ocean and introduced Islam to many Asian countries. In 1511,

Ⓔ _____

How to draw a cat
Start by drawing a circle, like this:

Ⓕ _____

These symbols tell the musician how long to play each note. This

Ⓖ _____

H_2O – This chemical symbol for water means that each water molecule contains two atoms of hydrogen and one atom of

Ⓗ _____

$875 \div 43 = 20.3488$

Listen and read

8 📼 Read and listen to the text about *The Five Ages of English*. Match the pictures with the paragraphs.

A 3........

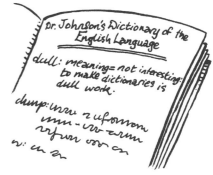

C ....

D ....   B ....   E ....

The Five Ages of English

1 Old English
From about the ninth century, the Vikings – who lived in what is now Sweden and Norway, began to arrive in the north of England. The language people spoke began to change. In the south of England, people began to translate books from Latin into English.

2 Middle English
In 1066, the Normans invaded England and French became the official language. Most educated people had to speak three languages: French, Latin, and English! At this time, English literature began to develop. One of the most famous writers was the poet Geoffrey Chaucer in the fourteenth century. His language is a little like the English of today.

3 Early Modern English
(1450–1750)
This period includes the time of William Shakespeare – England's greatest writer. By the end of the seventeenth century, great scientists, like Isaac Newton, wrote in English, not in Latin. The British Empire began, and the English language traveled across the Atlantic to North America, and across Asia to India.

4 Modern English
(1750–1950)
English was now a national language. The first dictionary – Johnson's Dictionary – appeared in 1755, and the first grammar books appeared soon after.
As the British Empire grew in the nineteenth century, English became a more international language. People began to learn English around the world. The first English language textbooks appeared in the 1930s.

5 Late Modern English
(from 1950)
Now, English language teaching is an important international industry. After World War II, the United States became the most important economic and cultural power in the world, and a world market in audiovisual communication began. CNN International began in 1989 and the Internet developed in the 1990s. English became a global language, with about two billion speakers.

Vocabulary booster: in an Internet café

9 **a)** Label the objects in the picture with words from the box.

screen	printer	~~chair~~	keyboard	mouse	CD-ROM drive	document	desk	modem	scanner

1	*chair*	3	....	5	....	7	....	9	....
2	....	4	....	6	....	8	....	10	....

b) 🖴 Listen to the pronunciation of the words on the recording. Practice saying them.

c) Write the words in one of the categories below.

Part of a computer	Connected to the computer	Not connected to the computer
screen	....	....
....	....	....
....	....	....
....	....	....

Pronunciation

Contracted forms

10 **a)** 🖴 Listen to the sounds and the example words below.

/ɑː/	father	art	car
/oʊ/	know	go	home
/ɜː/	work	girl	birth

b) 🖴 Notice the same sounds in these contracted forms.

/ɑː/	aren't	
/oʊ/	don't	won't
/ɜː/	weren't	

Improve your writing

Abbreviations on application forms (*Mr.*, *Mrs.*, *Dr.*, *n/a*)

11

a) Write the abbreviations for these words.

Mister	*Mr.*	January	....	October	....
Doctor	....	not applicable	....	December	....
Number	....	September	....	*et cetera* (= and the others)	....

b) Here are some other abbreviations you see on application forms.
Match the words on the right to the correct abbreviations.

1	Ave.	Street
2	e.g.	Avenue
3	kg	kilometers
4	km	North, South, East, West
5	Mon./Tues./Wed./Thurs.	*exempli gratia* (= for example)
6	N/S/E/W	Park
7	Pk.	Road
8	Rd.	kilograms
9	St.	United States
10	tel.	United Kingdom
11	UK	telephone
12	US	Monday, Tuesday, Wednesday, Thursday

c) Rewrite the following with abbreviations.

1 Mister James Hewson

   Mr. James Hewson ....

   ....

2 2 kilograms

   ....

   ....

3 63 Stamford Street

   ....

   ....

4 irregular verbs, for example *bring* and *buy*

   ....

   ....

5 Queen's Park Road

   ....

   ....

6 London South-West 7

   ....

   ....

7 10 kilometers

   ....

   ....

8 arrived in the United Kingdom from the United States

   ....

   ....

9 telephone number: 020 7939 3671

   ....

   ....

10 classes are on Tuesday and Thursday

   ....

   ....

11 January–March and April–September

   ....

   ....

Pronunciation table

Consonants		Vowels	
Symbol	**Keyword**	**Symbol**	**Keyword**
p	**p**et	iː	sl**ee**p
b	**b**oat	ɪ	b**i**t
t	**t**op	e	b**e**t
d	**d**o	æ	b**a**t
k	**c**at	ɑː	f**a**ther
g	**g**olf	ɒː	c**o**st
tʃ	**ch**ur**ch**	ɔː	hist**o**ric
dʒ	**j**eans	ʊ	b**oo**k
f	**f**ew	uː	b**oo**t
v	**v**iew	ʌ	b**u**t
θ	**th**irsty	ə	**a**bout
ð	**th**ough	eɪ	**da**y
s	**s**it	oʊ	ph**o**ne
z	**z**oo	aɪ	b**y**
ʃ	fre**sh**	aʊ	n**ow**
ʒ	lei**s**ure	ɔɪ	b**oy**
h	**h**at	ɪə	**a**r**ea**
m	**m**other	ɪ	h**a**ppy
n	su**n**	u	ann**ua**l
ŋ	you**ng**		
l	**l**ot		
r	**r**un		
j	**y**es		
w	**w**et		

Special signs

/ ˈ /   shows main stress

/ ˌ /   shows secondary stress

Published by
Longman Asia ELT
2/F Cornwall House
Taikoo Place
979 King's Road
Quarry Bay
Hong Kong

fax: +852 2856 9578
email: aelt@pearsoned.com.hk
www.longman.com

and Associated Companies throughout the world.

www.longman.com/cuttingedge

First published 2004
Reprinted 2005 (twice)

American English edition project managed by
Cambridge Publishing Management Limited 2004

Set in ITC Stone Informal
and Congress Sans

Produced by Pearson Education Asia Limited, Hong Kong
NPCC/03

ISBN 962 00 5632 9

The publishers and authors would like to thank Yvonne Gobert and Katherine
Stannett for their help and contribution in the development of this Workbook.

Photo acknowledgments

We are grateful to the following for permission to reproduce copyright
photographs:

Art Directors and TRIP for 8 bottom left; Corbis for 40 bottom left, 41 middle,
and 85 middle; Getty One Stone for 65 top, 65 bottom, 68 top right, and 68
middle right; Hulton Getty for 41 top and 50 middle; Image Bank for 8 top left;
Frank Lane Picture Agency for 65 bottom left, 68 top left, 68 middle left, and 68
bottom; Jeff Moore for 8 bottom right; Pearson Education for 49 left (Trevor
Clifford) and 49 middle (Peter Lake); Peter Newark's American Pictures for 41
bottom; PA Photos for 5 (all); The Photographers Library for 49 right; Popperfoto
for 14, 40 top right, 40 bottom right, 50 top, 50 bottom, 76 and 85 top;
Powerstock Zefa for 19; Frank Spooner Pictures for 40 middle right and 85
bottom; Woodfin Camp for 8 top right.

Picture research by Liz Moore.